W9-AZU-536

# Mother Mother

# James Stingley

# Mother
# Mother

CONGDON & LATTÈS, INC.

Copyright © 1981 by James Stingley

Distributor's ISBN 0-312-92543-3

Publisher's ISBN 0-86553-019-X

Published by Congdon & Lattès, Inc.
Empire State Building, New York, N.Y. 10001

Distributed by St. Martin's Press
175 Fifth Avenue, New York, N.Y. 10010

Published simultaneously in Canada by Thomas Nelson & Sons Limited
81 Curlew Drive, Don Mills, Ontario M3A 2R1

All Rights Reserved

Designed by Irving Perkins

First Edition

FOR LORALEE AND STROTHER

# Special Acknowledgments

To Eberhard and Phyllis Kronhausen, for the four years of encouragement and prodding that it took for me to face the reality that the story must be told.

To Richard Sidney Morris, for his guidance through the year it took to put this story on paper.

To Joan Barthel, for her friendship, which placed the author in Tom Congdon's hands.

To J. Stephen Sheppard, for his friendship, which placed the finished manuscript in Tom Congdon's hands.

To "Ria", whose moral and financial support contributed immensely to the writing of this story.

To my father and mothers.

*In memory of Strother Martin*
*Actor and friend*
*Sensitive creator*
*Most gentle of souls*

To preserve their privacy, the names of the two principal women in this account, and those of their families and friends, have been changed, along with the names of towns they have lived and now live in, and other identifying factors. The new geographical information is faithful to actual fact, merely somewhat transposed.

Chapter 1

The letter arrived on my desk in the metropolitan room of the *Los Angeles Times* on October 10, 1972. Mixed in with a small pile of other mail, mostly reaction to an investigative story I had just written for the paper, the envelope caught my eye because of its uniqueness. It was very expensive stationery—heavy beige paper, with embossed initials. And the postmark was Beverly Hills. Even though my byline appeared regularly in the *Times,* I did not receive fat letters from Beverly Hills. The only mail I had ever got from Beverly Hills was from the police department there, regarding an unpaid parking ticket my wife had gotten during a "Save the Seals" luncheon. So I picked this letter from the pile, observed with some interest the voluptuous penmanship, and carefully unsealed it, wondering which of my stories had prompted this response from a community that had heretofore remained unmoved by my prose.

Inside the envelope was a single sheet bearing only a few lines: "Dear Mr. Stingley, If you are the son of Royce Hunter Stingley and Edith Cook Stingley of Old Pine, North Carolina—would you please contact me at 271-8380." It was signed: "Mrs. David Dammeron."

I leaned back in my chair, lit a cigarette, and reread the note. It didn't tell me anything more the second time around. I had no recollection at all of Old Pine, a coastal town settled by Germans and Swiss in 1710. My mother and father, whose names Mrs. Dammeron had correctly identified in her note, had told me we lived there until I was two, but that we then moved south to Meadowbrooke, North Carolina, and maintained a home there from that point on. My mother was a secretary in Meadowbrooke, my father was a professional forester—hardly Beverly Hills material—and they had never mentioned knowing anyone west of Texarkana, Texas. One thing was certain. Whoever this Mrs. Dammeron was, she had no connection with me. I put the letter aside and began opening the other mail. I didn't know if I was going to call her or not. My parents and I had never been close and I had other things to do besides chat with some long-lost friend of a family that had really never been much of a family in the first place. Then the day city editor gave me a local assignment to pursue, and, when I finished that, it was time to cram my car into a space on the Ventura Freeway and crawl toward the San Fernando Valley.

The crawl was a pain. It always took an hour to reach Northridge, which, for almost a year now, I had been kidding myself was home. I hated the drive, and I hated the home, a three-bedroom ranch house with a brick, vine-covered wishing well in the front yard. It seemed to me so hopelessly middle-class-suburban that it made me wince. But it was where my wife had grown up and where she wanted to be. What kept me sane was that I spent at least half my time out of town on assignment for the *Times.*

The letter was still on top of my desk when I returned to the office the next morning. I read it again and looked at the telephone. I could feel myself soften. Dad had died eleven years before. Mom was getting old and many of her friends were dying. It wouldn't break my back to give this Mrs. Dammeron a call and let her know where Mom was. I dialed the number, less out

2

of curiosity than duty. I knew I'd feel guilty if I didn't call and she somehow turned out to be an old family friend.

"Dammeron residence," came the answer. I explained who I was, that I had received a letter asking me to call. "Oh! Just a minute," the voice replied in a lighter, excited tone. "I'll go get Mrs. Dammeron."

More than a minute passed, during which I wondered why my call had interested the maid. I lit a cigarette and swiveled my chair around, taking in the vastness of Otis Chandler's black and gray editorial domain. The huge *Times* building squatted over an entire city block in downtown Los Angeles, but it was from this one room that all the hard news was assigned, here that the stories were edited. When a reporter earned a seat in here, it meant he had reached the top of the journalistic mountain. From here he might be sent anywhere, to a Malibu brushfire or a war in Southeast Asia. Having a desk of my own in the city room was a kick, an accomplishment I particularly savored.

"This is Ria Dammeron," said a voice on the phone. It was the sort of voice you didn't often hear at backyard barbecues in the San Fernando Valley. The tone suggested—no, not suggested, but proclaimed—breeding, wealth, and a comfortable familiarity with a part of the world with which I had never been familiar or comfortable.

"This is Jim Stingley," I said in my best *Times* tone. "I received your letter and, uh, I am the son of Royce Hunter and Edith Cook Stingley. Now, who are you and what can I do for you?"

There was a pause on her end of the line, a discernible catch in her breathing. "Oh, well," she said, "I'm so glad you called. I saw your name in the *Times* and I thought to myself, Stingley. Would he possibly be the son of the Stingleys I knew when I was a little girl? The name is not that common, you know. At least, I haven't heard it or seen it since that time, and so I just thought I'd dash off a little note to you and find out."

She spoke fast, her voice almost lyrical and, it seemed to me, the slightest bit jittery.

"You've got me at a sort of disadvantage," I said. "My parents never mentioned knowing anyone in California."

Oh, dear, no," she said. "I haven't been in touch with them since just after you were born. They . . ." She paused. "Are they still alive?"

"My mother is. My dad died in 1961."

Another pause. "Oh, I'm sorry to hear that. He was such a nice man. But let me explain. You see, I knew your parents, quite well, actually, back in North Carolina when I was a little girl. Centuries ago. Tell me, are you married?"

"Yes."

"And where do you live?"

"In Northridge . . . that's in the Valley."

"Oh, yes," she said. "I'm familiar with Northridge. Terribly hot and smoggy there now. It used to be so beautiful when it was all orange and lemon and olive groves."

"I hate it," I said. "My wife's parents live there and that's why we're there. . . ."

"I wonder," she said, interrupting, "would you like to have lunch with me? Soon? I'd love to meet you because at one point, and you couldn't possibly know this, I played a minor role in your life."

"What kind of role?"

"Oh," she said, her voice regaining some of its earlier nervousness, "I gave you your name."

I paused that time. "I'm not sure I understand," I said.

"Well, I just did. Now, would you like to have lunch with me?"

I couldn't help laughing a little. Whoever she was, she wasn't shy.

"Am I funny?" she asked.

"Oh, no . . . no, ma'am," I replied. "I just don't get that many calls from nice ladies I've never heard of who say they named me. Now, you wouldn't be putting me on just a little bit, would you? I mean, what you're saying doesn't make a whole lot of sense."

This time it was she who laughed. "Well, I'm not going to tell

4

you another thing right now. You'll just have to have lunch with me and find out, won't you? Now. When shall we do it?"

I smiled into the phone. She was mysterious and she was flirtatious, and I was intrigued by both. "I can do it tomorrow," I said. "I'm not scheduled for anything after midday."

"Good," she said. "Let's meet at the Cave de Roys tomorrow at one. Do you know where it is?"

"No."

"The entrance is at Beverly Place and La Cienega. You can't miss it. Just announce yourself to the maitre d' and he will know you're my guest."

"Okay," I said, writing the information on a piece of copy paper. "I'll see you then."

She clicked off, and I slowly replaced the phone in its cradle. Weird. The whole thing was weird. How the hell could somebody you've never heard of have named you? I thought my father had named me after one of his favorite uncles. Perhaps my mother could've explained, but I rarely telephoned her and I didn't think to do so then. Instead I wondered what I should wear to this luncheon. Her voice and the name of this restaurant she'd suggested sounded like suit-and-tie. I owned one suit and one tie, the clothes I'd bought to be married in the year before. I guessed they would do.

Then another thought occurred. Why was I worried about what to wear? I had spent considerable energy at the *Times* breaking the "Old Gray Lady's" suit-and-tie code, as well as the no-beard-or-long-hair code. I was a jeans-and-workshirt journalist and proud of it. I did keep a tie and sports coat in my locker for extreme emergencies, like an unexpected invitation to lunch with Mr. Chandler in his executive suite. But I dressed as I pleased the rest of the time. The thought faded as I attended to the day's work.

The next morning I searched the closet for my suit and a clean white shirt to wear with it. Since I hadn't told my wife of the letter, the phone call, or the lunch date, she was astonished to see me dressing in my wedding clothes. I told her good-bye and walked out the front door, past the wishing well, and hopped into my topless TR-3. Backing out of the driveway, I saw her standing in the door, combing her hair, still staring.

As I drove out of the Valley, leaving behind the ranch houses with the campers and boats in their driveways, my thoughts turned to the woman I'd be meeting later. I wondered what she looked like. Probably old. She had to be old if she'd been a friend of my parents before World War II. Probably unattractive. I had this theory about telephone voices that had been proven true more often than not. Unattractive people always sound great on the phone.

At the *Times* I checked my mail and went to my desk to kill an hour before leaving for lunch. There were about forty reporters in the city room that morning. They kept looking over at me in my suit and calling out remarks. I ostentatiously ignored them, to their delight. Finally, I left for lunch early. I took the Santa Monica Freeway to La Cienega Boulevard and headed right, toward the Hollywood Hills. Half of me was fascinated by the whole adventure; the other half wondered why the hell I was even going through with it.

I spotted Beverly Place up ahead and turned left. I began to swing right, into the parking lot at the Cave de Roys, when suddenly my foot hit the brake. The parking lot resembled a Rolls-Royce convention. The parking attendant, who by this time was peering at me peering at him, was dressed in a uniform not unlike the Shah of Iran's. I took my foot off the brake, spun the wheel, and turned back out onto La Cienega. No way was I going to drive in there in my beat-up Triumph with the springs sticking out of the driver's seat. Two blocks further, I pulled over and parked.

Jesus, I thought, sitting there waiting for the time to make my entrance, whoever this woman was, she was way out of my frame of reference. Expensive cars are common in Los Angeles; I saw them all the time on Sunset Boulevard—Rolls, Mercedes, Jags. In good weather I would sometimes take an outdoor table at the Old World Restaurant on Sunset and try to see if I recognized any of the people driving them. But not even in my work—and

6

certainly not in my private life—did I frequent the restaurants and homes where cars like this were likely to cluster.

At one o'clock sharp I gave my beard a quick comb, then got out of the car and began walking toward the restaurant. As I walked, I adjusted and readjusted my tie and observed that I was getting nervous. The Shah spotted me and peered again. I flipped him a two-fingered salute and, very coolly, I thought, made my way to the entrance of the restaurant. I gave my name to the maitre d', who took note of my beard, my hair, and my three-inch-wide leather watchband and, with a strained smile, motioned me to follow him.

For no reason that I could figure, things began to get weird then. Some inner sense nudged me. Time seemed to wind down. I remembered walking down two or three steps into a cavernous room where the door was dark and rich, the tables spaced far apart. I seemed to see only men at these tables. They were speaking to each other softly. All sounds were muffled, lost in the dimness.

I noticed the maitre d' slowing his pace, waiting for me to catch up. I forgot about the soundless men in their cavern as we approached the door to a brighter, smaller section at the very rear of the restaurant. We entered and walked toward a woman seated at a table. She was staring at me. I stared back at her. Many steps before the maitre d' presented me to her, I knew she was the woman on the phone. I knew something else. I knew this was not going to be an ordinary lunch. The internal nudging had intensified when I saw her. It was a subtle feeling yet a strong one; I had never experienced it before.

I held out my hand to the woman, introducing myself. As our hands touched, the hairs on the back of my neck tingled. I seated myself and for a long moment neither of us said anything. In that moment I noticed her right hand locked around what appeared to be a vodka on the rocks. The knuckles were white from the grip on the glass.

"Well," she said, "did you have any trouble getting here?" She seemed uneasy.

"Uh—no, not really," I said, taking her in.

7

She seemed in her mid-forties, but even by L.A. standards, she was stunning. Her cheekbones were high and wide, her chin dimpled. Her eyes were electric blue. Her lips were supple and sensuous. Her hair was fiery red, styled dramatically, brushed back on the left and across and down on the right, sweeping just past the eyebrow. Her body, what I could see of it, was no less spectacular. Enclosed, but not totally, in a green silk dress, it recalled both Venus and the Amazons—big, but right in every proportion. For a country boy from the pocosin land of North Carolina who throughout his life had had an Anita Ekberg complex, she was decidedly a sight to behold.

Her jewelry stage-whispered her wealth. The diamond on her right hand was immense. On one wrist was a gold filigreed watch liberally sprinkled with emeralds, sapphires, and diamonds. On the other was a solid gold bracelet and a cocktail ring shaped like a water lily, with freshwater pearls blooming in every direction. The same large, baroque pearls were set in her earrings.

She broke me from my trance with a laugh. "Well, do you like what you see?"

I blushed, grinning. "I've seen worse."

"Now," she said, motioning to a waiter, "would you care for a drink?"

I ordered a double vodka on the rocks, she had a refill, and we were back again just sitting there looking at each other. I was waiting for her to say something—anything—that would explain what was going on. Her hand still kept a death grip on her vodka glass.

"I've been reading your stories for some time now," she said finally. "I really enjoy them."

"Thank you," I said. "I like doing them."

"Have you written any books?"

"No. I tried once, a few years ago. I found I couldn't write for the *Times* and do a book at the same time. It's hard to split your concentration—even if I had enough energy left over from the paper. I could quit, of course—but I guess I just haven't found a book idea interesting enough to yank me out of the Velvet Coffin."

"The what?" she asked.

"The *Times*. That's what they call her. The pay and job bene-fits are so much better than anywhere else that you think a long time before you leave that and take a chance on your own. I've heard plenty of my fellow reporters say, 'One of these days I'm going to write a book that's gonna . . .' But they never do. And they never will," I added, "as long as they have their Chandler grant."

She smiled. "Is that what they call it . . . their 'Chandler grant'? How amusing. I must tell Otis that one."

I laughed nervously. "You—you're a friend of Otis Chandler?"

"Oh, yes, I've know the Chandlers for eons. I mean, we're not close-close, because they are San Marino and I am Beverly Hills, and the two don't get together that often. But I'm particularly fond of Otis and Missy. His wife."

"Uh—well, you don't have to mention anything to Otis about what I just said. I mean, you know, it's just a little office humor."

"Oh, but Otis has a marvelous sense of humor."

"Yeah, but—uh . . ."

"Oh, don't worry," she said, laughing, "I was just teasing you."

"Good," I said with relief. "I think, uh, do you mind if I order another drink?"

"Please do. I'll have one too."

The drinks came, and we lapsed into another silence. Now that I knew she was a friend of my publisher, I was finding it hard to talk about anything.

"Should we order some lunch?" she said, motioning again for the waiter. "The food isn't that good here, but we should have something to offset the vodka."

I ordered a shrimp appetizer and a veal entrée. My hostess ordered a hamburger, rare. The food came, and we nibbled at it wordlessly. Suddenly I felt slightly foolish. I was a reporter, after all. I wasn't supposed to be reticent about asking questions. "Are you going to tell me about yourself," I said, "and about what you said yesterday on the telephone?"

She averted her eyes, concentrating on a bite of hamburger speared on her fork. "Well," she said, still not looking at me, "I live in Beverly Hills, I have a daughter by my first marriage. Oh, I don't mean I'm divorced. My first husband died. He was in manufacturing, had his own corporation back East. My present husband, Dave, is somewhat older than I. He was in shipping. Now he collects antique guns and restores them for the shows. They're really quite fascinating guns. One of them was owned by Thomas Jefferson himself—"

"What I mean," I said, cutting in, "is your connection with my parents and me. You said you named me. But so far, all you've told me is that you were a little girl in Old Pine and were close friends with Mom and Dad. How could you give me my name? Why wouldn't I know who you are?"

Her face turned hard. Then that expression disappeared, replaced by one of scrutiny. She cocked her head to one side and leaned toward me very slightly. "How," she said, reaching deep into my eyes with her own, "do you feel about me?"

The question froze in the air. It was an intimate question, and it demanded a serious answer from me. I took a cigarette from my pack on the table, lit it, inhaled, and blew the smoke down toward my plate. My eyes followed the smoke, watching it dissipate. I could feel her intensity penetrating me. I looked up from the plate, and our eyes locked.

"I'm attracted to you," I said. "I don't know exactly how to describe it. There's just something about you that keeps pulling at me. It's strange. It's very strange. I'm not sure what to do with it. I don't know. . . ."

She moved back from me, reached into her purse, and pulled out a cloisonné compact, edged in antique gold. She handed me the compact. "Open it," she said.

I undid the clasp and opened it. The only thing inside was a mirror. I looked back up at her.

"Look in the mirror," she said.

I looked in the mirror.

"Look at me," she said.

I looked at her, then back at my reflection in the mirror, then back at her. I saw her red hair, the blue eyes, the high, wide cheekbones. And then I looked back into the mirror at me, at my red beard, my blue eyes, my high, wide cheekbones.

"Who do you see?" she asked.

Her voice was still steady, but her eyes were afire now, and her body was fixed in a posture of expectation.

"I don't know," I said in confusion. "I don't know. . . ."

"I gave birth to you, Jim," she said seriously.

The statement hung in the air as though it had a life of its own. It echoed again and again, each time louder, until finally it was roaring at me: "*I gave birth to you, Jim.*"

I was still looking into her eyes, squarely. She didn't blink or retreat. As I stared, an image formed. Take away my beard, put its redness in my hair, and we were almost twins. Indeed, without question, this woman was my mother.

That I already had a mother did not cross my mind at that moment. Six words from a total stranger had invalidated that other mother in the seconds it took for those six words to register. I kept looking at her, watching more and more physical evidence fall into place, while, at the same time, feeling weights of incredible proportion breaking loose inside me. A giddiness began to envelope me entirely. My face, which I perceived to have been emotionless through all of what had just occurred, felt as if it were coming to life. I looked back down to the mirror and saw a smile forming on my face and then spreading into a grin.

"Yes . . ." I said slowly, looking up again. "Yes . . . you did." I laughed softly. "You . . . really . . . did. . . ."

Silently, we stared at each other. Her body visibly relaxed, and her face filled with a complex of emotions. I felt a rush, as if we had merged—incredibly, instantly, passionately, permanently.

Words poured from her, a million things she seemed to be saying, but none of them clearly. There was something about how my father had taken me from her when I was six weeks old and she was only seventeen. Images tumbled—rural, coastal North Carolina, poverty, a stepmother she hated, a father who never was home, then Old Pine, then West Virginia, then me, then not me, then just baby pictures, then suddenly no more

11

poverty, something about New York modeling, marrying a millionaire years her senior, birthing a daughter, losing her husband, inheriting millions, trying to forget me, her firstborn. Me, seeded by my father who took me away from her. Then, twenty-nine years later, seeing my name—the name she had given me—bylined on the front page of the *Los Angeles Times.*

And I remembered her saying that for three years she saw that name and for three years she kept hoping it would go away. But it didn't. For three years it didn't. Until finally, she said, it did go away. For weeks my name never appeared in the paper. Thank God, she thought, he's gone. I don't have to go through this hell anymore. And the next morning, sitting alone in her study, she took out those baby pictures that she had kept hidden from the rest of the world for all those years and slowly, tearfully, tore them into tiny pieces and dropped them into the trash. Later that same morning her maid handed her the *Los Angeles Times* and the name was there again. And she stared at it for a long, long time. And then she picked up a pen and wrote the letter.

"I knew then," she said, "that the time had come to give you your true identity." She reached across the table and took my hands in hers, gripping them tightly. I gripped back. A sensation swept through me like electricity. She smiled. "You know," she said, "I never forgot you. You've always been in my will."

"Will?"

"Yes. You see, Jim, I always knew, one way or the other, that I would find you. I kept that knowledge inside me; I couldn't share it with anyone. But I always knew I would find you."

"But you said you tore up my baby pictures and . . ."

"I said I knew I would find you. I didn't say I knew what I would do when I did find you." She radiated tenderness.

My mind was whirling. What did she mean exactly? How much was I in her will? How much of a will did she have? I answered my own question: there was no doubt in my mind that she had one hell of a will. What my mother was telling me was that I was going to be one rich son of a bitch.

She looked at her watch. "Dear God," she said, "we've been here nearly all day! I've got to go now, darling. I'm sorry. I didn't know what to expect and I guess I didn't expect that all this would happen as it has." She squeezed my hand. "Would you walk me to the car?"

We walked out of the restaurant together, and I sensed that she too was amazed and bewildered by our strange new bond. She began talking of her life in the very rich, highly social stratum of Beverly Hills . . . and how she expected me to be part of that. She was literally trilling—at last she had her son and could share with him what she had never before been allowed to give him. She wanted us to meet again, soon, so she could introduce me to her other child, my half sister, Janet.

As we reached the curb, the parking lot attendant drove up in a white and silver Rolls-Royce. He studied me again as he held the door open for my mother. We hugged each other tightly and she, smiling, got in the massive car and slowly drove away.

I stood on the sidewalk and watched her as she turned left on Sunset and disappeared in the direction of her world, the world of gardens and lawns that stayed an impossible green; air that seemed always clear and smogless; mansions that loomed high and huge and totally beyond the reach of mortals with tract houses, brown lawns, and wishing wells.

Then I turned and walked to my battered Triumph and drove the stretch downtown to the *Times*. The rest of that day was a fog. When I got home, I sat down with a drink and told my wife, Theresa, that I had met someone that day who was going to change my life.

"Who is she?" Theresa asked.

"I don't know who she is, really," I said. "I know what she is, though."

"*What* she is?"

"Yeah," I said. "She's the woman who gave birth to me."

I looked at Theresa now. She seemed baffled. "You—you mean that Edith isn't your mother? And you never knew?"

"No," I said, tears welling in my eyes. "Edith isn't my mother. And I never knew."

"Oh, God," she said.

"Do me one very big favor," I asked. "Please, under no circumstances, are you ever to tell Edith I know."

"You know me, Jim. I wouldn't do that."

"I know. I trust you. It's just so important that if she ever does find out, I should be the one to tell her. That is very, very important to me."

After Theresa went to bed, I sat there on the couch alone, sipping wine and smoking cigarettes until three in the morning. The thing that came back—that kept coming back and staring at me—was one cold, hard fact: nothing that had happened that day had surprised me.

# Chapter 2

Ria contacted me again two days later—another letter, again addressed to me at the *Times*. I quickly tore the envelope open.

"Janet and I share the same birth date," Ria's note began. "This was her 21st. Can you join us for cocktails on Wednesday? I will make other plans then, if you are in accord. I love you. Ria."

I immediately called her. We agreed to meet Wednesday in the Polo Lounge at the Beverly Hills Hotel. When the conversation ended, I sat at my desk lost in pure, sweet fantasy. If my sister was anything like our mother . . . my mind was soaring with the romance of it all. I envisioned being embraced and held by the two of them . . . fast, happy conversation, lots of laughter and squeezing of hands . . . and plans. Plans to have a party. Plans to go to some exotic place and nibble exquisite delicacies while we busily plotted out our future. Most of all . . . plans to be a family, a loving, caring, sharing family. I leaned back in my chair and grinned at the corniness of it all.

That Wednesday afternoon, back in my wedding suit, I made my way across town on surface streets. I didn't want to take the freeway because the top was broken on the old roadster and I was afraid my long hair would get too tangled. I wanted to look my absolute best.

In Los Angeles the Beverly Hills Hotel is more than a landmark; it is the cathedral of the stars. It is where anybody who was ever anybody in the motion picture business meets to have stunning lunches while waiting for his or her next stunning performance. And it is also where those same stars rent cozy bungalows to have torrid illicit affairs. I had never been inside the hotel. I would always drive by, as slowly as the traffic would permit, and just gaze at the pink palace, wondering who among the 'whos' were there. But on this day I entered and announced my name and Ria's to the maitre d' at the Polo Lounge, who, smiling, quickly ushered me into the semidarkness.

There sat Ria. She smiled and waved, saying something I couldn't hear over the din. The tables were packed closely together, each one fully occupied by human silhouettes that were talking loudly, either to each other or into telephones. Adding to the uproar was a midget uniformed in green and gold. He kept striding through the lounge yelling "Call for . . ." Every time the midget yelled and an arm shot up at a table or booth, a waiter would rush over and plug in a phone.

Somewhat disoriented by all of this, I sat down on Ria's right. She took my hand, nodded to her left, and said: "Jim, I want you to meet your half sister, Janet. Janet, this is my Jim."

I looked across the the table's flickering candle, past Ria's proud, big smile, at the figure seated there. A thin, wan face, framed by black, shoulder-length hair, stared cautiously at me with dark brown eyes that said nothing. The small hand that greeted mine was nearly limp and noticeably cold. Janet returned a shy half-smile, then retreated to a look of nervous caution. For a very long moment our table was a pocket of silence in a room full of noise.

"Now, Jim," came the sound of Ria's voice, "order yourself a drink and then tell Janet all about yourself and how you came to write for the *Times*. Janet has known about you for a long time." Turning to Janet, she said, "His is a fascinating story, dear. Absolutely fascinating."

Janet did not look one bit fascinated. But she smiled weakly at her mother's words . . . my mother's words . . . and she took a tiny, delicate sip from her glass of white wine. Ria was rapidly finding herself in the role of emcee—or referee, I wasn't sure which. She drained her glass of vodka and ordered another.

Determined to help Ria out, I did my best to entertain Janet with a light account of my past and my career, leaning heavily on what I thought were amusing items, but also tossing in, here and there, a few deliberate boasts about some of the more important stories I had covered. Ria was the perfect audience. She laughed at the funny lines, and managed to look impressed by my accomplishments; but Janet limited herself to faint smiles and withdrawn stares. Nervously, Ria tried to help Janet out with her responses. "Oh, now that is just a marvelous story," she would exclaim. "Isn't it, dear?" she would add, turning to Janet and touching her arm. Blinking her eyes, Janet would widen the thin smile a centimeter and nod her head.

I could see that I was getting nowhere with Janet. The question that was forming in my mind was why? One part of me wanted simply to say, "Please like me. We've got the same blood. We're brother and sister. You don't know how much it means to me to find I have a sister." But I could not imagine her responding simply and genuinely to those words. And the Polo Lounge did not seem the place to say them.

Ria was upset now, and, it seemed to me, disappointed. I wasn't sure which of us had disappointed her. Maybe, I thought, I've talked too much. Maybe my jokes weren't funny and my career talk was a lot of rank bragging. The meeting at that point ended. Ria glanced at her watch, saying that both she and Janet had to "run" in order to get ready for a dinner engagement. The three of us walked out of the lounge and into the light of the lobby. As we went out the front entrance, I noticed Janet's dress. And I remember thinking how odd, that she, at twenty-one, dressed like a matron—in a long gray skirt and an off-white blouse that buttoned at the neck—while Ria dressed like a girl at party time.

We stood waiting for the attendant to bring Ria's and Janet's cars, and Ria made another attempt at the union of her blood.

"Well, this has just been so delightful," she said, hugging Janet with one arm and me with the other. "Now, let's see. Why don't we throw a little party at my house one evening . . . oh, why not this Saturday? And that will give the two of you a chance to really get to know each other better. Is that all right?"

"Sure," I said hopefully. "I'd love it." I smiled at Janet and she smiled back wanly, again nodding her head.

"Fabulous," proclaimed Ria, hugging us tighter. "Fabulous."

Driving home to the Valley that afternoon, I remembered feeling numb as I stood there watching Ria depart in her Rolls and Janet in her Jaguar. The numbness was more a feeling of dislocation, as though I was standing somewhere in between a life that wasn't and one that was yet to be.

The life that wasn't had begun when I turned thirty. I was living on the 17th floor of an 18-story high-rise that had a view of Santa Monica to the right, Venice to the left, and the Pacific Ocean about 150 yards west. By Southern California standards, it was the perfect place for a bachelor with a good salary. The pickup bars of Marina Del Rey were only minutes away and the beach lay at my feet, where I could jog, surf, or get a tan. The apartment complex itself provided an Olympic-size swimming pool, a deli, a large laundry, and an endless assortment of single, attractive female tenants—models, actresses, stewardesses, nurses, schoolteachers. All of them apparently dedicated to pursuing the sexually liberated singles life at the beach, even if they had to live two and three to an apartment in order to afford it.

I should have been enjoying myself, and I was. Then my mother wrote me a long letter from North Carolina, wishing me a happy birthday and launching into a sad complaint about how lonely life was without my dad and how she sure wished I could do something about that by finally marrying, settling down, and providing her with a grandchild. It wasn't the first time she had brought the matter up. Whenever I visited her, she always managed to slip that subject in—usually as we were saying good-bye. This letter made me feel particularly guilty because I had just turned thirty. Back in the society where I'd been raised, and where my mother still lived, a thirty-year-old bachelor wasn't a "catch"—he was a disappointment to his family. I knew my mother felt let down, and maybe I was feeling a little of that loneliness myself, even in the midst of the singles delicatessen that was my apartment house.

So I shaped up. I met a girl in the laundry room who met all my mother's requirements. She was well-mannered, well-educated, mixed nicely at parties, was attractive, pleasant, a good cook, a lover of antiques (as my mother was), and an elementary grade school teacher who knew how to make a dollar stretch. Following a short but intense courtship, I took her to North Carolina, where she and Mother fell in love. Shortly after that, we took another trip to North Carolina where, in the living room of my mother's house, we were married. That she and I had totally different interests, except for good food and wine, and were sexually incompatible besides, were things I didn't even consider. I had done my duty. And when she suggested moving from the clear air of the beach to the smoggy depths of the San Fernando Valley because it would be cheaper to live closer to where she taught, and because her family lived there, I did my duty.

Now . . . now I knew I was going to undo that duty. I had been leaning in that direction anyway, before Ria had entered my life. But as I drove home from the Polo Lounge that afternoon, the how and when of our separation totally occupied my mind. My wife was a very nice woman and I wanted this to be as painless for her as possible. The irony was, at this moment when my life was turning upside down, I needed Theresa for the first time. She knew I was confused and she was being very understanding.

The Saturday of Ria's "little party" Theresa spent the entire morning at her hairdresser's, getting another dose of whatever it was that kept her black hair gold. When she got back, she said hello and disappeared into the bedroom. I was absorbed in a football game on television, but finally I realized that she had

19

been in there for a very long time. "What are you doing?" I yelled. No answer. I got up and walked to the bedroom door. She was standing at the end of the king-size bed with hands on hips, biting her lips as she surveyed four dresses laid out on the bed. "Hello?" I said.

"Which one should I wear?" she asked, her eyes still on the dresses.

"You're asking me?"

"No, I'm asking me," she said.

"Oh," I said, and went back to the living room. I had never seen her so concerned about what to wear.

Finally she emerged, dressed in one of the outfits. I started to tell her she looked nice. "Just keep notes," she said. "There's more." An hour and five more dresses passed before me. Finally she emerged in her jeans and a T-shirt. "Well, which one?" she asked.

"I like the long green slinky one," I replied.

"You always like the long green slinky one," she said, walking to the bar and pouring herself a glass of wine.

"Nervous?" I asked.

"Yes," she said, draining the glass and pouring it full again. "Of course I'm nervous. I'm a schoolteacher in the Valley, and I'm going to a party in Beverly Hills where there's going to be God knows how many· 'beautiful people' who are all going to stare at me and say, 'Who the hell brought the schoolteacher from the Valley?' "

"No, they won't," I said. "Ria's not that way. Everything is going to be fine. Just relax."

"Jimmy," she said, "you have no idea how women look at women in Beverly Hills. If you're not wearing some designer original you might as well be wearing pedal pushers from the Good Will."

I looked at her standing there. "Come here," I said, "and sit down beside me."

She came to me and settled on the couch, crossing her legs under herself, and stared across the room. Her newly done hair fell down over her shoulders.

"You look great," I said, stroking her hair.

She turned her dark eyes toward me. "I wish I felt I did, Jimmy," she said. "I wish . . ." Her voice trailed off.

"What?"

"Oh, nothing," she said. "I guess I'm just nervous . . . about a lot of things."

I kept stroking her hair. "Look," I said "you don't have anything to be nervous about. I mean, hell, I'm not nervous."

A look of exasperation quickly came to her face. "You're not nervous because you don't know how to be nervous, Jimmy. That's the one thing that you don't seem to know about yourself and it's also the one thing that bugs me about you."

"What are you talking about?" I remembered how nervous I'd been as I'd entered that restaurant a few days before.

"I'm talking about you, dammit. I mean, a few days ago a woman comes up to you and tells you that she's your mother. I would probably flip right out if that happened to me. So would anybody else. But not you. No, you come home and you act like, 'Hey, guess what happened to me today?' You accept things without question that would absolutely stun anybody else."

She shook her head. I lifted my hand from her hair and lit a cigarette. I was becoming a little angry. "What was I supposed to act like?" I asked.

"I don't know, Jimmy. I really do not know. I guess what I'm trying to say is that you are just real insensitive to most things around you. Little things never impress you. You don't even notice them. Unless they bother you. And God only knows what it takes to bother you. Sometimes I just marvel at you and think, 'Gee, I wish I could walk through life the way he does.' But then sometimes I feel a chill about it. It's almost as if you're some kind of method actor that lives his life from this big scene to that big scene. You have a really scary way of focusing, or locking yourself in on things. It's scary because if I don't happen to be in that particular scene, then it's as if I don't exist at all."

By now I had stopped hearing what she was saying. I glanced at my watch and put out my cigarette, grinding it slowly to death in the ashtray. I was thinking about Ria . . . and how we'd better start getting ready. I didn't want to be late.

"Look," I told my wife, "now's not the time for you and me to get into a heavy duty analysis of how weird I am. I know how weird I am. And sometimes you like me anyway."

She looked at me and shook her head, letting out a long sigh. "Okay," she said. "I'm going to go get ready."

Since it was a long drive from Northridge to Beverly Hills, Theresa and I decided to leave early, just in case we got lost looking for Ria's house. Ria had called the *Times* and given me detailed instructions, but neither Theresa nor I had ever been in that area . . . or so we thought. But as we turned left, just past the Beverly Hills Hotel, both of us realized we had indeed been here before—as tourists.

"Holy shit!" my wife whispered as we slowly wound our way up and around streets we had traveled one Sunday afternoon. "She lives here?"

I swallowed and, grimacing, nodded. My underarms were growing moister. We were dwarfed by the immensity of everything. These houses were not merely mansions, they were the realizations of elaborate fantasies. Behind electric iron gates and hand-cut stone walls, we saw Italian gardens and marble statuary and waterfalls. The lushness of the foliage was overwhelming. And as we slowly proceeded, almost hypnotized, I was particularly struck by the observation that everything was in place. The lawns were all precisely cut to the same height, and not a blade of grass was leaning in the wrong direction. The streets were immaculate and totally deserted. No cars were parked on them, no people or dogs or cats walked along them. Everything was behind the walls and gates. Everything and everybody.

We found the street that Ria lived on and turned. More of the same. My wife said nothing, absorbed, I would later learn, in the idea that wealth of this sort was now related, in some way, to me. As for me, I felt as if I was shrinking. The deeper into this world I went, the smaller I felt my body grow until it seemed I was an insect looking up at a redwood tree.

We finally reached Ria's address and I pulled up short of the entrance. I wanted to take in and permanently record what would be my induction center . . . the anteroom to my new life. It was, indeed, a sight to behold. Unlike most of the houses we'd passed, Ria's home had no gates or walls. Instead, it sprawled invitingly behind an elongated horseshoe drive that curved through a garden of flowering azaleas and sculptured shrubs. The house itself was colonial, not plantation-style colonial with white, towering columns, but a more understated Beverly Hills colonial. I could not help but notice that, in the midst of all the other fantasy estates we had passed, Ria's home was distinctively southern.

Theresa nudged me. "Don't you think we'd better go in?" I looked up the curved drive again. No cars were parked there yet, but Ria had said there would be ten or fifteen other guests at the party. I eased my wife's station wagon to the curb and parked.

I looked at the golden-handled door, wondering anxiously if, once inside it, I would be accepted, if I would finally find a home. I pushed the doorbell and a melody chimed faintly. By the time the short tune was finished, the door was opened by a black woman dressed in a maid's white uniform. Her eyes twinkled dark brown as she looked up at me and smiled. "You got to be Jim," she said, her smile deepening. "I'm Ella." We shook hands and she held mine firmly in hers for several seconds. "My, my!" she laughed. "My, my!" Then she noticed my wife and invited the two of us in. "Mrs. Dammeron is in the kitchen helping to get dinner ready," she said, taking us from the marble-floored foyer through a sitting room. It was dark and furnished with a lot of cut crystal and an endless variety of what I figured were called objects of art. "She said for me to take you to the bar and let you fix yourselves a drink," Ella said, "and then she'll join you in a minute."

As we walked through the sitting room I paused, my eyes drawn to a huge photograph of Ria that hung above the fireplace. Theresa brushed up against me, looking at the portrait too. "Is that her?" she whispered. "She's beautiful."

I agreed. She was beautiful. She had posed on a formal, high-backed chair covered in a silvery raw silk. She was leaning forward, confronting the viewer with her body. But it was the expression on her face that struck me. It left no question that this house was her universe and she was the center of it.

The maid led us on, down a step into a large room that seemed to stretch itself out in every direction. In one corner was the walnut-paneled bar, which Ella gestured toward as she departed to what I assumed was the kitchen, hidden away by double swinging doors. The bar was fully stocked, expensive brands. I fixed a gin and tonic for Theresa, a vodka on the rocks for myself, and then studied the room in which we found ourselves.

To my left, deep-cushioned couches and chairs, covered in warm, flowery prints, were grouped around a large circular glass coffee table; twenty people could be accommodated easily there. Beyond that was a lanai where, surrounding another sitting area, a tropical forest seemed to be growing out of great indoor pots. Near the lanai, a long glass dining table was set for dinner. Sliding glass doors opened onto a garden. Set in the spacious, well-tended lawn were a large swimming pool and two large patios, bordered by shrubs and flowering plants and orange, lime, lemon, grapefruit, and loquat trees.

Beyond the dining table I saw another sitting area, more formal. And there was still another dining room, this one with crystal chandeliers looming over a long, highly polished antique table. Surveying all this from the bar I thought to myself, *My mother—er, Edith—should see this.* Then I shook off that thought.

I looked at Theresa. She was still checking out the rooms. She looked at me, sighed, and shook her head in disbelief. "Do you believe this?" she whispered. "White carpet! I hope I haven't left any footprints."

Just then the double doors to the kitchen burst open and in strode Ria wearing a large apron over her evening dress. Pearls shimmered and diamonds glittered. Her hair had been freshly done and her eyes were shining.

"Hello, dear," she said, leaning over the bar to give me a kiss. Then she turned. "And this must be Theresa," she said. "Well, darling, welcome to the family."

Ria extended her hand, and Theresa timidly put her hand in Ria's. "Your home is beautiful," she said.

"Why, thank you, darling. You're so sweet. I rather like it myself." She turned to me. "Jim, darling, I've got to dash away and touch myself up before the others get here. My husband will be out in a minute. He's running late as usual. You two just relax and have another drink. If you need anything, just ask Ella." She gestured toward the kitchen. "Nice to have met you, dear," she said, looking at Theresa. Then she disappeared down a hallway. Theresa's eyes followed Ria until she was out of sight. "I don't believe it!" she whispered.

"What?"

"I swear, Jimmy. If you shaved your beard off, you two would look like twins."

I smiled. But I was thinking of something else. I had seen Ria's look at my wife and noted how intense and penetrating it had been. In one second she had evaluated Theresa and I could hear her thinking, *Sweet, but definitely not right.*

The door chimes rang then, and people began filing into the foyer. As the first chime sounded, Ria came out of her dressing room and signaled for me to come to her. Quickly she ushered me into the large room and closed the door. "Now, Jim, dear," she whispered, "I hope you won't mind, but the people who are coming tonight don't know you are my son. They have been told you're my brother, and they'll buy that because our ages are close enough and physically we're dead look-alikes. Later, when things get more settled, we'll clear the matter up. But right now, if you would go along with it, it would make things a lot easier on me."

She spoke quickly, but so forcefully that I was persuaded she was right, this was the most prudent move for the moment. It was her game anyway, I thought. She was the coach. I was the rookie. As I nodded my agreement, she locked her arm through mine and led me back to the bar where a man and a woman in their forties were talking to my wife.

"Peter! Cory!" Ria exclaimed, "How beautiful you could come! I want you to meet my brother, Jim Stingley."

The couple stepped forward. "Hello, Jim," said the man. "I'm Peter Kemp and this is my wife, Cory. Ria just told us her incredible story about how you two hadn't seen each other in thirty years and then suddenly she recognized your name in the *Times*. I think that's just wonderful, just great."

"Oh, it's fascinating!" said Cory. She was a striking woman with dark hair and fair skin. "But," she said, laughing, "it's not surprising. We've learned not to be surprised at anything concerning Ria. She's totally and delightfully unpredictable."

Indeed she was. My wife's eyebrows had risen when Ria introduced me as her brother, but I just shrugged my shoulders and turned to meet Ria's husband, who had just joined us. Dave, as Ria called him, was a gracious, soft-spoken man. He told the Kemps that he had admired my pieces in the *Times* long before he'd learned I was his "brother-in-law."

Within half an hour the other guests had arrived, including Janet and her fiancé, Ronald Hamner. Janet was much warmer toward me than she'd been at the Polo Lounge. She smiled and hugged me, and I hugged back. Her fiancé was another matter. As we waited for Janet to introduce us, I looked at him and knew two things. I knew he'd been told I was Ria's son, and I knew that we instantly disliked each other.

"I understand you write for the *Times*," he said in a low, affected tone that was trying hard to sound superior.

I nodded and sipped my drink, trying to control my negative feelings for Janet's sake. But he was staring at me oddly, his dark eyes glittering.

"Do you like it there?" he asked.

"I love it there," I said, trying to sound enthusiastic."

"They don't have a very good book review section," he said, his eyes bearing down on me. "You would think that with all the money the Chandlers have, their book review section could at least approach the quality of the *New York Times*. I take the *New York Times*. Far superior. In every way."

"I don't think so," I said, "Certainly in terms of good writing and reporting and news coverage, we're as good as they are, if not better."

"You think that, do you?" he said condescendingly. "That's a pity."

Excusing myself, I rejoined Theresa, who looked as if she could use some help in her conversation with a silver-haired broker and his wife. When I glanced back at Ronald, he grinned, still looking at me in his cold, superior way.

Dinner was announced shortly afterward. I was pulling out a chair for Theresa when Ria tapped me on the shoulder.

"Dear, Theresa goes over there," she said, pointing to a certain chair. "Just look at the place cards and you'll know where to sit."

Sure enough, there were little white cards at each place.

As I searched for my seat I also took notice of the elaborate table settings. Each person had three glasses and twelve pieces of silverware.

I finally found my seat, which was next to Ria—who sat at the head of the table. Janet sat across from me and Dave was to my immediate right. Down the table, toward the end, was Theresa. Beside her was Ronald.

Ella, who had silently been joined by a butler, began serving. First came caviar, accompanied by small glasses of chilled vodka. Thereafter followed six more courses, among them smoked trout and baby veal with lemon sauce.

"When we know we're coming here for dinner," Cory Kemp said to me, but loud enough for Ria to hear, "we don't eat all day. Ria is the best cook in town, dear. The absolute, very best!"

I nodded, my mouth full.

Ria, obviously delighted with the attention, fluttered. "Well," she said in an affected, lilting tone, "I do like to think of cooking as an artist thinks of a finished canvas . . . a portrait of culinary creation, expression." This was her "British" accent, which I had noticed by now she never used when she was talking alone with me.

Throughout the meal, Ronald, Janet's fiancé, kept his gaze on me. I avoided it, trying to stay in touch with Janet and Ria. I did well with Janet, but Ria seemed launched into some orbit of her own, and I seemed to be the only guest not delighted by her performance. But I pretended I was. It was her show.

As it turned out, I talked most that night to Dave. In his early sixties, he was a retired shipping executive who had been, years before, a leader in American nautical design. He had married Ria in 1970, three years after her first husband died and two years after his first wife's death. Nowadays, he told me, he was content to spend his time reading and "puttering" with his collection of antique guns. He was quiet and sincere, charming in his own way, but as I watched Ria out of the corner of my eye, as she entertained the entire table, I couldn't imagine how the two of them had gotten together. Although Dave had distinguished himself in his profession, here in Beverly Hills Ria was unquestionably the star.

After dinner Ria summoned everyone to the semicircle of sofas and chairs in the living room, where Ella served liqueurs and cordials. When everyone had a drink, Ria suddenly turned solemn. She placed her glass down on the table and settled herself back on the couch, folding her hands together as if in prayer, tilting her chin up. She closed her eyes and seemed to go into a trance. The guests fell silent. Finally she opened her eyes. Tears were welling in them.

"You know," she said, "tonight is a most special occasion. It is, actually, the end and the beginning." Her eyes panned slowly from person to person. "It is the end of a life's separation of two souls of the same blood—myself and"—she looked over at me, reaching out her hand to take mine—"my dear, sweet, darling brother. Our lives began together, yes. They began together in the shadows and folds of the Great Dismal Swamp. And we"— she looked straight into my eyes—"were like delicate little swamp creatures, full of love for each other, afraid, really, to be without each other. And yet . . . that was the very thing that came to be."

Ria's head, then her shoulders, began to sway gently now. Her eyes settled on a point in the middle distance. "There . . . there was this song," she said, "that we used to sing together. It began," and she began singing, in a champagne soprano, "Amazing Grace."

I looked over at Janet, but she was examining a spot on the

white carpet. I bit my lip and tried to look nostalgic and pious. Everyone else—including Theresa—seemed hypnotized. Ria sang only one verse of the song, then began to speak again.

This was the first of many "Ria shows" that I would attend. She played out the scene, regaling the group with what was basically a pack of fibs concerning "our" childhood. I followed her leads, affirming at the appropriate times. But what I was really doing was absorbing impressions of my mother. I had never seen such an animated, flamboyant character. Nor had I ever seen such a charming liar.

It was nearly 2:00 A.M. when Theresa and I left for home. When I announced our imminent departure, Ria began to tease me. "Why, little brother, surely you're not leaving now?" she said. "The night has just begun!"

"You've done me in, sis," I told her. "I've got to leave Monday for an assignment in Montana, and I'm going to need all day tomorrow to rest up for the trip."

"Well, honey," she said, lapsing into a southern accent, "you go on now and get your beauty sleep." Turning to Theresa, she said, "You'd better drive, darling. And tuck him into beddy-bye. I just didn't know the poor boy would wear out so quick." Even though she was smiling and hamming it up with the accent, her tone of voice told me she would expect more of me in the future. I was too tired to speculate on how much more.

As we drove home, Theresa talked excitedly about the entire affair. A very gregarious person, she had been delighted and amused by all of it.

I didn't say anything. As I drove, my mind kept rerunning the evening. She had introduced everyone but Ronald to me as "family"—people she considered closest to her. With the exception of Janet and Dave, this "family" consisted of her lawyers, her accountant, her investment counselor, and their wives.

Peter Kemp was obviously her number one family member. I had been embarrassed by the way she fawned over him, but his wife hadn't seemed to mind. Peter was head of the law firm that administered Ria's first husband's trust fund—the money spring from which she drew the sustenance for her expensive style of life. But it also appeared that Peter, a handsome man with an air of quiet confidence, genuinely cared about Ria. I decided I liked him every bit as much as I disliked Ronald. But it was Ria who really occupied my mind. She was so much larger than life that I still had trouble bringing her into focus.

I let out a long sigh. We were back in the Valley, in our driveway, by the wishing well. Theresa had fallen deeply asleep and I sat watching her for a long moment. I wondered if she was unhappy with our marriage, too—if her outburst that afternoon was just the tip of her anger. I had no way of knowing, really, but I did know one thing: I was closer than ever to asking her for a divorce. For some reason, our evening at Ria's had made that clear.

Chapter 3

Over the next several months, I continued to try and live my life with Theresa as usual. Ria often invited us to dinners and small parties at her home, or asked us out to dinner with her and Dave. Sometimes Janet and Ronald would join us unexpectedly; Ria was clever enough not to let me know in advance that he would be there. I became accustomed to trying to ignore him while looking for chances to talk to Janet. She was still shy and still did not seem willing to accept me into the family, but we talked often enough, and I felt happy that at least we were both making an effort.

Eventually I began to see Ria more on my own. We would meet for lunch at her house or at the Bistro on Rodeo Drive. At home I was her son. At the Bistro I was her brother. The masquerade bothered me, but it became a minor concern while I increasingly concentrated on how to end my marriage.

In the spring Ria and Dave began to travel a great deal—to London for a month and a half; to Jackson Hole, Wyoming, for a few weeks' fishing; to a friend's ranch near Santa Barbara; to New York for some plays and shopping. I was traveling a lot, too, for the paper, and although I occasionally spoke to her on the phone, October faded into mid-November before I saw her again. It was the week before Thanksgiving. She had called me at the *Times* and asked if I could drop by after work. Her voice was edged with concern.

When I arrived, Ella greeted me warmly at the door and told me Ria was momentarily tied up on the telephone. "Mr. Dammeron is in bed," she said. "He's not feeling too good today. Would you like to come in and have a cup of coffee with me?" I followed her into the kitchen, and we sat at a small table.

"How long have you been working here?" I asked.

"Oh, I've been with Mrs. Dammeron fifteen years," she said. "Yep. Fifteen whole years."

"How is she to work for?"

"Oh, she's fine. We have some disagreements every now and then, but then, most folks do that. But she's good to work for. She's kind and generous and she treats me like a member of the family . . . which"—Ella laughed—"sometimes is good and sometimes it isn't so good." She leaned toward me, her brown eyes solemn. "But I wanted to just tell you something, while I had the chance."

"What's that?"

"You've just made her the happiest woman on this earth."

"I have?"

"Oh, honey, I know who you are. She doesn't know I know, but I do. I knew who you were the minute I laid eyes on you. Ain't nobody in this world more her son than you are. Rest of them folks believe you're her brother. But uh-uh, not me. I seen the look in her eyes when you called her back that first day.

"But I just wanted to tell you that. We keep it a secret 'tween you and me. But I did want to tell you that since you come along she been like a little girl around this house. And I never seen her be that way before. You have made her so happy by accepting her."

"Well, it really wasn't that hard for me to accept . . . but thank you."

"Anyways"—she smiled—"I just wanted to tell you. Now
. . . uh-oh, I believe I hear her coming."

I winked at Ella and sipped my coffee. Ria came into the
kitchen and hugged me tightly around the neck.

"Well, Jim!" she said. "I thought I was never going to see you
again."

I smiled at her. "Yeah, well, it was just a matter of getting our
planes to land here at the same time."

"God, I know it! Well, we should be here for a while now."
She paused. "Listen, why don't we fix ourselves a drink and talk
in the library. I need to discuss some things with you."

I prepared drinks for both of us, and we went into the library.
The room served as one of Ria's offices. The other office was her
dressing room. In each room she had large antique desks. The
dressing-room office, I learned, was where she did all of the bill
paying for the house. The library desk was where she conducted
any business regarding the trust fund she administered. Ria settled herself in a huge upholstered chair, and I sat at her desk in
a leather armchair that swiveled.

Ria was looking grim. "Jim, I hate to burden you with this,
but I've just got to talk to someone or I'm going to go stark,
raving mad."

"What's wrong?"

"Dave is a very sick man, Jim. I think he . . . he's going to die
very soon." As she said the words, tears came to her eyes.

"I—I don't understand, Ria. He looked healthy as a horse the
last time I saw him."

"Well, he wasn't," she said. "He's been having back pains for
some time now, very severe ones. He kept telling me that it was
just an old injury. He was going to a chiropractor for treatment.
I asked him to go to a real doctor, but until recently he refused.
But I smell death on him, Jim. I've been smelling it for a while
now. And . . ." Her voice broke and she started crying. I went
to her and put my arm around her. She held me tightly, her body
shaking as she sobbed. Finally she spoke again, and this time her
voice was bitter.

"I'm too young to bury a second husband, dammit! For twelve

long years I played nursemaid to a dying man. I spent a decade of my life trapped here under this roof, never able to go anywhere or do anything except minister to him. You have no idea what that's like, watching yourself grow old and lonely because your husband refuses to die and refuses to let you out of his sight. And now Dave's dying, Jim. When we were in Wyoming the pain got so bad I was finally able to get him to a real doctor. And . . . well, he has cancer. He thinks it's curable. But I know the smell of death, Jim. And now I can look forward to God knows how long of sitting here and watching him die." She began sobbing again. "It—it's just so goddamn unfair!"

I held her, not quite knowing how to react to what she was saying. On the other hand, I flinched at what seemed to be monumental self-pity on her part. I didn't know how to understand it. I didn't know if it was justified or not. And on the other hand, I felt sad about Dave. Sadness about him, and sadness for her.

Finally she stopped sobbing and lifted her head from my shoulder. She reached for a tissue to wipe her eyes. I stood up. "Are you going to be okay?" I asked.

She nodded. Slowly her composure returned. She took a sip from her drink.

"Can I do anything to help you out, Ria?" I asked.

She sighed, shaking her head. "No, dear, there's really nothing anybody can do. Not for Dave, anyway."

When I finally got home that evening, Theresa was angry, and I didn't blame her. I had forgotten to call and tell her I would be home late. But when I told her Ria's news, her anger dissolved.

"It sounds like she needs you," she said. "It sounds like you came along for her at just the right time."

"I don't know what it sounds like," I replied. "But she really is torn up about Dave." I didn't tell Theresa the whole of it, Ria's anger over Dave's illness, her tone of "How dare he do this to me!"

Theresa and I spent Thanksgiving with her family. Dave was not totally bedridden, and Ria had arranged for a quiet family get-together at Dave's winter home in Palm Springs. She had invited us to come along, but understood when I explained that we were already committed to Theresa's parents.

After Thanksgiving, I began to drop by several times a week after work and visit with Dave. Theresa seemed to understand. She knew Dave and I liked each other, and she knew also that my visits comforted Ria. It was a strange time. I had never before watched anyone die. As Dave's weight ebbed away, so did his strength, but he tried to be bright and upbeat when I was with him. His bravery, once he had accepted his fate, was touching.

During these visits, I saw the toll being taken on Ria. At first she cared for him herself, bathing him, padding his body against bedsores, even diapering him. Finally she hired a live-in nurse. Still, she was emotionally exhausted from it all. When she and I did have a chance to sit down and talk, there were a lot of silences. What talk there was mostly came down to one thing. We were simply waiting, Ria and I, for Dave to die.

His death came more quickly than expected. In the second week of December, he was taken to the hospital. The next day he was gone.

Theresa and I attended the funeral. It was a simple, brief service at a Presbyterian church in Beverly Hills. Dave's body was cremated and—at his request—the ashes were taken up in a private plane and scattered over the sea. Theresa and I took Ria home, where, along with Ronald and Janet, Ria's "family" was gathered for a quiet wake.

At one point, Ria asked me to follow her into the kitchen. "Jim," she said, "I'm going to need you to help me a little bit now, if you can. I'm so afraid of being alone."

"Don't worry," I said. "I'll do whatever you need for me to do."

"Oh, now I don't mean that I want to take your time with Theresa away," she said. "But . . ."

"Like I said," I told her, kissing her on the cheek, "don't worry. You've got me."

She kissed me on my cheek. "Thank you, darling. Thank you.

I don't know why I have such a fear of being alone. But I do, particularly in this big house."

When Theresa and I returned home that night, I sat up late thinking about Ria. In that moment we had spent in the kitchen together, she had seemed like a little girl, a child who was afraid of the dark. More important, the child had said that she needed me. I made a decision.

The next morning was a Sunday. When Theresa awakened, I told her a lie—that Ria had called early, depressed and upset, and that she wanted me to come by and talk to her. I drove to Ria's home, parked my car in her driveway, and rang the doorbell. After a minute passed, I rang the doorbell again. Finally, a little brass plate in the door raised and I heard Ria's voice exclaim, "Oh! Jim!" The door opened. She was wearing a frilly green dressing gown, and I was afraid I had awakened her until I noticed that her makeup was already on.

"Good morning," she smiled. "What a surprise!"

"I hope I'm not too early," I said, giving her a hug. "But I need to talk to you."

"Well, come on in to the kitchen. I just made a fresh pot of coffee. Have you had breakfast?"

"I'm not hungry."

"Is there anything wrong?" she asked.

"I just wanted to ask if you would help me with a problem I have," I said.

We sat down at the kitchen table, and she poured coffee for both of us.

"What's your problem, kid?"

"I want to divorce Theresa."

She looked across her raised coffee cup at me. "I knew that. I was just wondering when."

"Well, I didn't know when myself until last night. But I sat up all night thinking about it and this seems the right time. I just wondered if Peter Kemp . . . handles divorces."

"He's only the best divorce lawyer in the entire nation," she said. Then she rattled off the names of several famous actors, agents, and businessmen whose divorces Peter Kemp had presided over.

"Well, this one will be pretty small potatoes by comparison, but I don't know any other divorce lawyers. Do you think he'd do it?"

"Yes," she said. "Yes, he will. And Jim, I must tell you that I think you are doing the best thing. Theresa is a wonderful girl, very pretty, very sweet. But she's not for you. That's not her fault or your fault. But don't worry. Peter's office will take care of it whenever you let them know."

"Well, I'm going to let them know pretty soon," I said. I spent perhaps two more hours with Ria, talking about how I very much wanted to make the divorce as easy as possible for Theresa. I didn't see us as adversaries, and Ria agreed to help me make that clear to Peter Kemp.

I drove back to the home in the Valley. Theresa was on the telephone with her best friend when I walked inside. I fixed myself a drink and, when she hung up, I looked at her for a long time without saying anything.

"What's wrong?" she asked.

"Sit down with me on the couch," I said. "I've got to talk to you about something." We sat on the couch. "I don't know how to say this," I said, "but I'm afraid I want a divorce."

She looked at me and shrugged her shoulders. "I know. I've known for months."

"I'm sorry. . . ."

"Oh, Jimmy, you can't help it. I haven't said anything because I haven't known what to say. At first, I thought, well, maybe it will pass. But it just got worse. And you kept putting more and more distance between us . . . so finally, dammit, it just came down to waiting for you to say it."

"Are you mad at me?"

"No. Maybe I wish I could be. But I'm not. The whole thing is too understandable. I saw it start to fall apart when we moved here to the Valley. Then when Ria came into your life. . . . Does Ria know?"

"No," I lied. "She knows I haven't been happy with married life. But, no, I haven't told her I was going to ask for a divorce."

We both sat for a moment without speaking.

"I guess we'll be separating then," she said. "When?"

"Well, we might as well get the word out now," I said. "But it's only two weeks until Christmas . . . and I'd like it if we could spend that time together before you . . ."

"Well, shit!" she exclaimed, smiling at me while tears began running down her cheeks. "I'll have to say this. I really enjoyed it while it lasted."

I looked at her and put my arms around her. We hugged each other tightly. I felt a surge of guilt run the length of me, but I also felt a great sense of relief.

"Can we stay friends?" I asked.

"We've never been anything but friends," she said wryly. "Do you know that we've never even had a fight?" She laughed. "Everybody I know envies us because we're the perfect couple!"

For me, that Christmas gave new meaning to the term "mixed emotions." Ria invited us over to exchange gifts with her and Janet. There we all were, everybody but Janet aware in one way or the other of the divorce, and we all acted as if this was the first in a long line of family Christmases.

We gave Ria a stereo cassette player to hook up to her sound system. I had selected a silver and crystal caviar service for Janet. These presents had almost bankrupted us, but we were determined that they be as nice as the gifts we knew we would receive.

Janet's gift to me was a set of first editions—autographed books of poetry by John Boyle O'Reilly. Inside the first book was a simple note: "Jim, I am glad you are my brother." I looked up at Janet. For the first time, she seemed to look at me with love. It was a moment I wished I could isolate, take somewhere, and make it last longer.

Ria's gift to me was a heavy, gold Swiss watch, the cost of which I couldn't even imagine.

Then came Ria's gift to Theresa. The box was very large and Theresa was getting excited as she wrestled it open. Inside was a full-length coat of silver fox, a beautiful Beverly Hills creation that must have cost Ria thousands of dollars. It blended perfectly with Theresa's blond hair and brown eyes. All the way that night, Theresa kept caressing the coat and marveling at it.

"And that's not all," I said. "Tomorrow night you and I are going to have a party. We're going to the fanciest place in Beverly Hills."

"For our divorce party?" She laughed.

"Yeah . . . right."

We reached the home with the wishing well and Theresa tried her coat on again while I turned on the radio and fixed us drinks. Then we sat down on the sofa together, Theresa still wearing the coat.

"How am I going to look tomorrow night? I think I'll wear my green dress, my long green dress."

"You'll be the knockout of the place, babe. You think your mother and dad will like it?"

Theresa laughed. "I should tell them about the separation at the same time they see the coat."

"You do look so good in that."

"It's so gorgeous! You know, the funny thing is, I've never been the type to say that I wanted a fur coat or that I wanted . . ."

"No, you've never asked me for anything."

"I mean, I see fur coats on other women and they are very nice. That's all. You see them a lot. All the women in that bracket have that coat. The thing is, this one is so different. I've never really seen one like this! You want to know what it is? It's me."

"Exactly."

"It's Theresa and Jim."

"It's Theresa."

Within a week, the divorce was in Peter Kemp's hands. Theresa had agreed to the quickest divorce possible and was contesting nothing. I felt lucky and happy that our parting was so simple and dignified. Probably it would have been that way in any case. But months later I realized that, just to make sure, Ria had bought me some Christmas insurance—the fur coat. I was shocked, then angry. I reminded myself that I hadn't known in advance what she was planning to do. And in the end I admitted to myself that although I myself would not have done it, in my heart I was glad Ria had.

When I told Edith about the divorce, she was shattered. "But why, Jimmy? Why?" she said over the telephone. "You two were so perfect together. Theresa is the nicest, sweetest girl you could ever hope to find! Can't you reconsider this?"

I told her no.

"This just breaks my heart," she sobbed. "I don't understand how in the world you could do this."

"You act as if I was doing this to you," I said angrily. "Don't you care about how *I* feel? Don't you care that this divorce is a very sad thing to me? I mean, I know you love Theresa, and you can keep on loving her. She's your friend and always will be. But I don't love her, and I can't stay married to a someone I don't love. Doesn't that mean a goddamn thing to you?"

"Jimmy," she said coldly, "I think you are doing a very silly thing. You haven't given Theresa a chance. You don't ever give anybody a chance. Once you make up your mind, that's it. I don't understand how you can treat people this way. I just don't understand it at all. You've done the same with every other girl that I've liked. You keep them for a while and then you dump them. But this . . . this just breaks my heart."

Even when she was over 2,000 miles away, she still could make me feel guilty. I fought the feeling hard. "I'm sorry, Mama," I said, "but I've got to do what I've got to do. I can't live that kind of a lie."

Theresa and I separated during the first week of 1973. I had explained my situation to my boss, metropolitan editor William F. Thomas, and he let me take a week's vacation and seven days owed me from the year before. I quickly found a one-room efficiency apartment in Hollywood about halfway between the *Times* and Ria's house. I moved some of my possessions there, and Theresa agreed to hold the rest until I found a more permanent place.

During the first week, while I was getting settled in my new location, I spent little of my time with Ria. She and Ella were busy sorting out Dave's belongings and making decisions about what to do with them. It was at the end of that first week that Ria and I finally found our respective tasks accomplished and were able to get together alone. It was a Saturday afternoon. Ria had invited me over for cocktails and dinner.

When I arrived, I parked the car as I always had—on the curved drive in front. I was starting to get out when she opened the front door and told me that from now on I should bring the car on through the carport to the inside parking compound. I liked that. As I clicked off the ignition, I felt that at last I'd arrived.

Ria met me at the back door. She was wearing white slacks and a filmy green blouse that was opened at the top so that just the slightest curve of her cleavage was exposed. She had a drink in her hand and a smile on her face.

"Well, alone at last," she said, stepping toward me and kissing me on my nose. "And I've got an absolutely marvelous dinner planned—if you like champagne, caviar, and prime rib."

"Oh, I think I can force it down," I said, kissing her on the cheek. We walked inside to the bar and I stepped behind it to fix myself a drink. As I selected a glass and Ria seated herself on a bar stool, I felt a stir of excitement—something to do with this new circumstance. For the first time neither of us had a husband or a wife to come between us. Now she was the most important person in my life, and I was the most important person in hers. It was the situation every child wants most, and now I had it.

"Here's to our new lives," I said, raising my glass.

"Yes," said Ria, her eyes looking at me in the same, shimmering way they had the first day we had met. "Here's to our new lives. . . ." She stopped mid-sentence, taking my hand and pressing it in hers. "And most important, here's to your new life. I just hope you won't mind if I help you prepare for it."

I squeezed her hand back. "I'd mostly be delighted, ma'am," I said in my most southern way.

She laughed, clearly responding, blushing ever so slightly.

"Well, now the first thing we have to do," she said gaily, "is to get you a wardrobe. You could use a few things, couldn't you?"

"I've got one suit and one pair of dress shoes and one white shirt," I said. "That's all I've ever needed before, apart, that is, from my jeans."

She almost shuddered. "Well, darling, that will just not do. You said you have some time off from work. How much?"

"I have all of next week."

She pursed her lips and gazed away thoughtfully. Then she turned back to me. "All right. I know exactly what to do. Can you give me some of your time next week, beginning Monday morning?"

"Sure."

"What I'm going to do is have Veronica, my dressmaker, come over Monday morning. She will take you over to Rodeo Drive and get you some decent wearing apparel." Ria winked at me. "After all, dear, if you're going to keep up with me, you'll have to look your best."

I smiled and shrugged. I had played more than a few games in my life. I'd never played dress-up because I always found better ways to spend my money. But since I was more or less putting my future in Ria's hands, if she wanted me to have new clothes, I would have new clothes.

"By the way," she said, "you'll like Veronica. She's about your age and she's beautiful. Actually, I don't know what I would do without her. She takes care of all of my clothes. She'll fix you right up."

"In what way?" I grinned.

"Why, Jim!" she exclaimed, her eyes laughing. "How could you talk like that in front of your own mother?"

"Sister," I smiled back.

"Oh, that's right," she said, shaking her head and laughing. "I must remember to keep that straight."

Ria prepared the dinner while I walked around the estate with a drink in my hand, feeling very much like a member of the leisure class. After dinner we sat in the library and talked about things we had never had a chance to talk about before—music, poetry, the theater. Ria told me about the clubs and organizations to which she belonged, all of them associated with charities. As we talked I realized that, at least on the subjects of music and poetry, I knew more than she did. That helped relieve an uneasy feeling I had been having all evening that perhaps I was stepping, however willingly, through Alice's looking glass.

Monday morning I reported as ordered to Ria's. A Corvette was parked at her front door as I drove into the compound. Ella greeted me at the back door and was offering me a cup of coffee when Ria came in with Veronica.

Veronica took one look at me and turned to Ria. "My God! He's your twin!" she said. Then she turned back to me, her blue eyes flashing. "I think I'm falling in love with him," she said, winking at me. "Can I keep him, Ria?"

Ria laughed. "You just dress him, dear. Maybe later I'll share him with you."

"Okay, lover," Veronica said to me, grabbing me by my hand. "Let's go get dressed for Mommy."

Ria coughed, almost choking. "He's my *brother,* dear," she managed to say.

"Oh, my God, of course!" said Veronica, shaking her head. "Why did I think he was your son? He couldn't be, unless you had him when you were ten years old." Ria and Veronica laughed, Ella laughed, I laughed.

Veronica roared off toward Rodeo Drive with me clutching the dashboard and wondering if she had never heard of the Beverly Hills Police Department. As she drove, she talked about the miracle of Ria's reunion with me. "It couldn't have happened at a better time," she said. "Ria's been through hell with Dave's death. All she needed was to have to play nursemaid to another dying husband. I've never seen a woman have more bad luck with marriage. But"—she smiled at me—"you came along at just the right time. Ria's ecstatic about you." I smiled and nodded, watching the road come at me faster than my nervous system would have preferred.

"Ria said you write for the *Times,*" Veronica continued. "What sort of writing do you do?" I mumbled something about investigative reporting and human interest stories as she shot across a six-way intersection through a maze of other cars that seemed to be coming at us from all sides. "Oh," she said. "I just read the comics and Joyce Haber," she laughed. "The rest is depressing. I can be depressed on my own, I don't need any help. By the way, which do you want first—shoes, shirts, or suits?"

Before I could begin to decide, she pulled into a parking lot, and we walked into a very plush, quiet shop that, as far as I could tell, sold only shirts. Veronica led the way and I hung back as she went straight to a salesman and spoke to him. The man nodded, reached for a tape measure, and walked up to me. He took measurements of my neck, chest, shoulders, and arms, jotting down each figure as he went along. Then he motioned to Veronica and the two of them went over to some sort of catalog.

"Okay," she said, "let's have two of those and . . ." Her selection went on until it totaled about fourteen shirts. "What are your initials, hon?" she asked me across the room. "J-M-S," I replied. Then she walked over to a display of shirts and picked eight, all white, all long-sleeved. Four of them had frills on their fronts and little black beads where the buttons should have been.

"These will last until they get your order ready," she said to me as the salesman placed the boxed shirts into a bag. She turned to the salesman. "When the others are ready," she told him, "have them delivered to this address as soon as possible."

Back out on the street, I peeked into the bag. "Some of these are formal shirts, aren't they? I don't have a tux."

"We'll get you one, darling," she smiled, "after we get you some shoes, socks, and ties."

"Oh," I said. "Uh, why didn't you get ties at the shirt store?"

"Because I can get the same tie for half the price at the place we're going to get your shoes," she said. "Their shirts are worth the money. But why spend forty dollars on a tie when a fifteen-dollar one will do?"

I almost swallowed my tongue. Forty dollars for a necktie? My whole suit had only cost $100 and I had thought that was outrageous. "I see your point," I told Veronica.

From the shirt store we went to the shoe store, and Veronica selected seven pairs of patent leather loafers, including one pair in white and another in burgundy. Two dozen pairs of socks. Two dozen ties. I had stopped being surprised by now. I simply stood or sat, as required, and watched Veronica choose the items and sign the bills. I had no idea how any of it would look on me; my notion of color in clothing ranged from light blue to dark blue. But I did cringe at the white shoes.

I followed Veronica like a large, obedient puppy for the next two days until everything on Ria's list had been obtained or ordered. A tailor measured me on Tuesday for a tuxedo, a navy blue dress suit, and five sports coats with accompanying trousers. I reported back to him on Thursday for a second fitting and picked up the finished products that Saturday. As I hauled the last load up to my apartment, I began to think that I would need another apartment just to store this bonanza of apparel.

I hadn't seen Ria during the week with Veronica. She and Janet were spending a few days at the Palm Springs house that Ria had inherited from Dave, but I was to have dinner with her Sunday night. So Sunday afternoon I cleaned my old clothes out of the closet and unpacked and hung up the new ones.

For that evening, I selected the navy blue suit, an off-white shirt, a navy blue tie with tiny gold dots, dark blue socks, and black leather loafers. After showering and giving my beard and moustache a slight trim, I sprinkled myself with Aramis cologne, donned the shirt, which had a diamond-shaped, raised monogram on the left cuff, and then put on the rest of the ensemble. It was only then, when I tried to button the cuffs, that I noticed they were of the French variety. And I had no cufflinks. Somewhat panicked, I drove around Hollywood until I found a shop and bought a set of cheap, gold-plated ones.

When I entered Ria's parking compound, I spent several minutes checking myself out in the rearview mirror. I was nervous. Really nervous. It bothered me that suddenly I was worrying about my appearance. I never had, before I met Ria. But my overriding feeling was the hope that I was going to please her.

I rang the back doorbell and Ella let me in. "My, my!" she

said, grinning. "Uh-huh. She's in the library right now waiting for you.

I walked through the double doors into the living room and toward the library. I had to admit to myself that I had never felt so comfortable in a suit. Everything fitted. That in itself was a totally new experience. When I reached the library, I squared my shoulders and made my entrance. Ria was sitting in the big stuffed chair, beautiful in a long dress that emphasized her bosom—as, it seemed, did every dress she owned. I stopped and stood still as she looked me over.

"Come here," she said. On a table beside her was a set of diamond and gold cufflinks. She took my cheap ones off and threaded the new ones in. Then she stood up and stepped away from me.

"Turn around," she said.

I turned slowly around.

"You look absolutely gorgeous, Jim. You look perfectly divine. Now that's the way you ought to look all the time, instead of wearing those hippie clothes. I can't tell you how handsome you are."

Something inside me rankled at her reference to my old clothes, but that was stilled by her praise of what she saw. "Well, thank you, my dear," I said. "Will I do?"

She laughed. "You'll do just fine. Now," she said, her expression turning serious, "please do me one favor. Do not tell Janet that I bought you these clothes."

"Why?"

"Well, I'm afraid that Janet, as sweet a girl as she is, might feel the wrong way if she learned about the clothes. Okay?"

"I guess so."

"Oh, don't worry about it. Time will take care of it. We just have to be a little careful right now."

I nodded. "Well, are we ready to go?"

"Go? Oh, no, dear. Tonight is just a dress rehearsal. We'll eat here. Ella's fixing dinner and I bought some absolutely delightful caviar for you and me to snack on. But don't worry. We'll be going out a lot soon. I can't wait to show the new Jim off."

Back in my apartment that night, somewhat buzzed by champagne, I held my own dress rehearsal. The bathroom door had a full-length mirror, and I opened the door so that the mirror faced the living room. Turning every light in the apartment on, I dressed in each new outfit. When I had one on, I would then go out the front door of the apartment, turn, and then reenter, striding smartly to a point on the carpeted floor that was just far enough from the mirror to catch my full image. Stopping there, I would posture and flex and turn, fully and totally enthralled with the "new" Jim. The tux was the best. It was maroon with black velvet lapels and pant stripes. With it I wore a custom-made, peach-colored shirt with a mass of ruffles down the front, a black velvet bow tie, and shiny maroon patent leather loafers. To me, it was all beautiful.

Standing there in that outfit in front of the mirror, I turned my body slightly to emphasize my shoulders. A smug, casual smile played across my lips. Pretending I was at some important function, cocktail in hand, I began an imaginary dialogue, conversing with a woman of striking beauty who had seen me from across the room and had made her way over to me.

"Hello," she said, looking me straight in the eye.

"Well, hello," I replied, looking her straight in the eye.

"And who are you?" she asked, with a very interested smile.

Saying nothing, except with my eyes, I reached inside my jacket and withdrew a creamy embossed card that read, in raised letters, STINGLEY. I placed the card in her hand, letting my fingertips lightly touch hers.

She looked from the card to me. "And what do you do?" she asked.

"Do?" I replied. "Do? My dear, I *do* nothing." I smiled wryly. "But I do it exceedingly well. . . ."

The next morning was Monday—time to put away the toys and get back to the reality of working for a living. Usually, all this required was splashing water on my face, brushing my hair and beard, donning a pair of jeans, a denim workshirt, and a pair of scuffed shoes, and heading on in. But on this morning I spent an unprecedented hour preparing my appearance. I chose the same outfit I'd worn at Ria's, completed with the diamond and gold cufflinks.

I grinned as I drove to work. There was hardly anything I took more delight in than creating a disturbance in the *Times*'s staid metropolitan room. I had shocked them first by growing my beard, then by not wearing a coat and tie, then by letting my hair grow shoulder length. After I had established that persona, which someone once referred to as "our staff slob," it became accepted and, to some degree, imitated. Now, I thought, it was time to shake them up again.

I knew I was on the right track when, as I walked into the *Times*'s front lobby, the security guard who usually glanced over and waved me on by, stopped me as I tried to stride past. "May I help you?" he asked. I pulled my *Times* identification card and flashed it. "Oh, Mr. Stingley! I didn't recognize you."

I smiled and walked to the elevator that took me to the third floor. Tugging my cuffs to make sure the diamonds showed, I walked through the door that opened directly in front of the city desk.

"Morning, Jack," I said to the day editor who, cigar smoke billowing, was bent over a small heap of copy. He looked up, did a double take, and softly exclaimed, "Jesus!"

I turned left without responding and walked slowly past the rows of desks manned by reporters flailing away at their typewriters. As I moved along, it seemed that with each step I took a typewriter slowed and stopped, until by the time I had reached my desk the din of clicking and clacking had almost entirely ceased. Looking at no one, I unfolded the morning edition of the late final and pretended to read. After a few minutes I let my eyes steal over the top of my paper and, sure enough, half the staff was still staring at me.

Finally, it was too much for them. Eric Malnic, an assistant city editor, and three reporters strolled over to my desk. When they arrived, I looked at them blankly. "All right, Stingley," said Malnic, an inquisitive smile on his face. "Who died?"

The following Saturday, Ria asked me to join her for the day, beginning with a luncheon. I arrived this time in a light green herringbone sports coat, darker green trousers, another of the custom-made shirts, and still another pair of new shoes.

"You look absolutely marvelous!" she exclaimed, walking around me with her hands on her hips as she examined her creation. Tilting her head to one side, she lapsed into her very best southern accent, "Stick with me, kid. Yo' mama is gonna show you the way!"

I laughed, and we hugged. This time the hug was a little closer and a little longer than usual. She shivered the least bit and slowly backed away. "My goodness," she said. "You've given me goosebumps.

"Well," she said, breaking the tension, "let me get my purse and we'll be on our way." She walked into her bedroom, got her purse, and returned, handing me a key attached to a ring that was attached to a leather piece stamped with the initials RR. "Would you mind driving?" she asked, as she pressed the button that opened the garage door.

I looked at the sleek, silver Rolls-Royce. "You trust me?"

"You gotta learn sometime, kid." She smiled.

With me at the wheel, we drove west on Sunset Boulevard, through Pacific Palisades and down to the Pacific Coast Highway. The windows were up and it was like driving a soundproof room. Ria placed a cassette in a slot and suddenly the car was filled with light classical music. "How do you like the car?" she asked, as she leaned her back against the door and looked across at me.

I kept my eyes on the curving road. "It's beautiful. It feels kind of heavy when you take a sharp curve, or when you come to a stop. But it ain't shabby. Basically, it's a four-wheeled fantasy. What kind of mileage does it get?"

"Darling," she said, smiling at me, "who cares?"

Over cocktails and lunch at a Malibu beachfront restaurant, Ria talked about our new life. "How would you like to be my escort for a while?" she asked.

"In what way?"

"Well, in this town, when a woman's husband dies, there's not a ready supply of worthwhile male companionship. So I thought as long as you're not going with anyone right now, you could escort me to dinner occasionally, and to a few parties. Someone is always giving a party somewhere. It would give you a chance to meet some absolutely fascinating people. And I wouldn't have to worry about what anyone was saying about my escort because they all know now about my little brother."

"Sure," I said. "I'd be crazy to pass up dating you."

Midway through the lunch, Ria became earnest. She looked at me for a while, not saying anything. Then she took my hands in hers.

"Now, Jim," she said, "today I want to tell you how very special you are to me. I love you so very much. And I told you when we first met that I wanted to give you some of the things that I know you've never had. . . ."

Her tone had changed now, and once again I was hearing the haunting, maternal sound of her, the voice that mixed joy and regret. Touched, I interrupted her. "You already have," I said. "You've given me my mother."

"Oh, no, dear," she said. "Edith is your legal mother. I can never be your legal mother. . . . I'm just the woman who gave birth to you." She stressed the word "legal."

"But," I said, looking puzzled, "but—"

"Oh, dear," she said. "I'm just saying I can't be your legal mother because you've already got one. But you are my baby, my firstborn, and that's all that really matters.

"Now," she went on, smiling, "let me get back to what I was about to say. I want to give you some things. One of the things I want to give you is a little money. Not much. As you know, I live on a trust fund which is worth a lot, but I am not allowed free access to the whole amount. But," she said, "I have an excellent financial consultant, and every now and then we manage to do well in the stock market.

"Anyway, dear, I want you to have this gift. And I want you to join me for dinner tomorrow night for the presentation of it. Peter Kemp will join us, and he'll explain everything regarding the gift.

50

"And Jim," she said, squeezing my hand, "I have told Peter that you are my son."

I smiled. "You mean I'm not your brother anymore?"

"Not to our immediate family," she said. "Socially, we'll still pretend for a while. All of this is just going to take some time. But," she said, winking, "we're going to have an absolute ball doing it."

She chatted all the way to her home about things "we" were going to do. I listened at the same time wondering why she had felt the need to stress the term "legal mother" at lunch. It was more fun to think about the next night's dinner and the gift.

I picked Ria up at dusk the next day. The Bistro was our destination, and as I headed the Rolls east on Sunset, Ria explained to me that the restaurant did not have very good food but that it was "the" place to be in Beverly Hills and that it was owned by a friend of hers.

"Every restaurant we've been to hasn't had good food in your opinion," I remarked jokingly, "and everyone else thinks they're the best restaurants in the city."

"But dear," she said solemnly, "how could they have good food—compared to my cooking?" I looked over at her. She gave me one of her winks. We both laughed.

As we stepped inside the restaurant she was greeted by the maitre d'. He did a big hello, then ushered us into a wildly decorated room with rows of tables along each wall. The maitre d' pulled out a table and we were seated, facing the length of the restaurant and a crowd of diners.

"We're being stared at," I whispered in Ria's ear.

"Of course, darling," she whispered back. "They all know who I am, but none of them know who you are, and they are beside themselves because they don't know." She chuckled. "I love it!"

Peter and Cory soon joined us, and we all ordered cocktails. Peter sat facing me. He smiled warmly, shaking his head as he looked from me to Ria and then back to me again. "Jim, Ria told me just two days ago about you," he said. "I must say, what she has done is a most courageous and admirable thing. And I must say that, you, Jim, are an outstanding person in your own right.

I've been reading your very fine reporting and writing in the
*Times* for three years now, and I can't tell you what a surprise
it was when Ria told me about you—that you were really her
son. It's an amazing story.

"Now, Jim," continued Peter, "Ria wishes to give you a small
present and I think it is most generous of her to do so and, at
the same time, very loving and very appropriate."

"It's a little nest egg, kid," Ria said, ruffling my hair. "And
you can thank Peter for it. A fellow tried to pull a fast one on
me financially, and Peter, bless him, took the crook to court and
won."

Peter laughed, shrugging off the praise. "Thank you, Ria," he
said, and turned back to me. "Anyway, Jim, my office will get
this to you next week. It amounts to $15,000 in cash and in some
stocks."

I almost swallowed the olive pit I was chewing.

"I am sure, Jim," Peter continued, "that you will agree with
me that Ria, in doing this, is showing you just how much she
cares about you. We all care about you, Jim. You're part of the
family now."

"Oh, look at him blush!" laughed Cory, looking over at me.
"You're so cute, Jim Stingley, I can't stand it." She made a mock
growl and flashed her teeth as if she were going to have me for
dessert.

I just sat there dazed by it all. It wasn't until I had escorted
Ria back home, hugged, kissed, and thanked her, and was back
in my apartment that it finally registered. Fifteen thousand dollars! Goddamn! Whew! Fifteen thousand dollars!

The next day at work I wasn't worth a damn. All I could think
about was that money. I had never in my life seen more than a
thousand dollars in a lump sum, and that hadn't even been mine
to keep. I had borrowed it to make a down payment on about
two acres of land Edith had inherited from my father back in
North Carolina . . . two acres of land and a log cabin that I had
wrongly assumed she would give me as my birthright. She had
insisted I buy it from her instead.

Peter's office worked quickly. The stocks were transferred to my name, and the cash part of the present was in my hands by the next week. It came to ninety-five hundred dollars. The first thing I did was buy a bright red 911E Porsche, complete with sun roof and wraparound stereo. The car had 5,000 miles on it, but it looked brand, spanking new. The second thing I did was find an apartment in Malibu and buy a king-size bed for it. Even though my Porsche was used, and even though my apartment was on the mountainside rather than on the beach, I didn't care. I had arrived, man. I had arrived!

Chapter 4

It was not too long before working at the *Times,* which had been my salvation before Ria, was suddenly becoming something of a drag for me—a duty that I had to perform so many hours per day before heading to Beverly Hills and the pleasures I was finding there. But I bore the duty for two reasons. No alternative had been offered to me. And Ria seemed to take great pride in introducing me as a "front page writer for the *Los Angeles Times.*"

I was her full-time escort now, and suddenly found myself being greeted most warmly by the owners and maitre d's of the most fashionable places in Beverly Hills. Often this attention seemed fawning, but since Ria seemed very much to enjoy it, I suppressed any criticism I had. And as time passed, I came to like being fussed over myself. I liked it most particularly when other patrons would nearly break their well-dressed necks to see who was receiving such special attention.

Until now I had been content merely to get a reservation at a good restaurant—and, with luck, a seat that wasn't right beside the kitchen door. Now I was learning that I had been living the life of a peasant. Ria was my teacher. I learned that the "best" table was the one that was the most exposed to the eyes of the patrons. I learned that an evening out was made or broken on the basis of whether the owner made an appearance at your table. If the owner actually sat down with you for a moment, that was a bonus that earned you the envy of the onlookers. I learned that one did not ask the price of anything on the menu, nor did one ever use cash to pay the tab. One simply signed the bill and the total, including tip, was figured by the captain or maitre d'.

I learned my lessons so well that now, during my work week at the *Times,* I forsook the company cafeteria and reserved a table for myself each day at the best downtown restaurants. I was beginning to take a real fancy to myself, and most assuredly to my new life. Ria had even helped me furnish my Malibu apartment, choosing—and paying for—furnishings that I could never have afforded on my *Times* salary of $20,000 a year.

To my faint dismay, I found myself beginning to press her for more money. "You know," I told her one day, "hanging around with you is beginning to give me a real inferiority complex."

She simply said, "Oh?"

"Yeah. I mean, I make a salary that's in the top 10 percent of American wage earners and, if you subtract my income tax and social security payments, I couldn't pay even your restaurant bills for six months."

"But Jim," she said, "we don't eat out all that often."

"That's what I mean," I said.

"Well, I guess you're just going to have to work harder and make more money, aren't you?" she said with what I interpreted as mock seriousness.

"That really wasn't what I wanted to hear," I said, sighing heavily.

"I know what you wanted to hear, darling," she said with a smile.

I laughed. But part of me was silently saying, "Then do something about it, dammit."

Of course, she was doing a lot about it. When I was with her, she picked up every tab down to and including the dollar tips for the parking lot attendants. Whenever we went out, she would hand me a fold of money to take care of such matters. The fold always exceeded the necessity by a great deal. And if I tried to give her change, she would refuse, saying she probably owed it to me anyway for some thing or another when she had been caught short of cash. Since she was never, in fact, caught short, I always had a surplus of pocket money.

Still, there was something inside me that was ever so slightly chafing at the fact that Ria was not carrying me completely. I wanted to tell her how tired I was, how completely burned out I was from struggling to make it in my own world. And how much I saw her as my rescuer. But I didn't. I knew I ought to appreciate what she was doing for me.

When I first bought the Porsche, I had driven out to Janet's house in Trousdale one Sunday morning. I had hoped she would join me for a ride to Malibu and, perhaps, lunch.

She answered the door in a houserobe and a rather cautious smile.

"I didn't wake you, did I?"

"No," she said. "I was just reading the paper. Come on in."

It was my first look at Janet's own home and I was more than a little curious. Her taste in decorating was much more conservative than Ria's, and more to my own liking. The browns and oranges, deep reds and light tans of her home were warm and comfortable. It was a one-bedroom house, but very roomy. Sliding glass doors opened to a patio with an uninterrupted view of a wild, down-sloping canyon.

"Coffee?" she asked, leading me to the living room.

"No, I'm fine," I replied. "I just finished breakfast. Listen, I was wondering if you'd like to go for a ride over to Malibu and maybe have lunch." I grinned. "I want to see if you like my new toy."

Janet's eyes flickered. "Toy?"

"Come on outside and see it," I said. "I just got it yesterday."

I led the way, and when we reached her driveway, I proudly gestured at the gleaming Porsche. "Well, whaddya think?"

Janet looked at the car for a long moment. Her face was immobile. "It's nice," she said in a flat tone.

"Well, how about it?" I said. "Ready to see how she drives?" Still looking at the car, Janet stood there, her coffee cup seemingly frozen in her hand. "No . . . I—er, have a luncheon I have to attend." She looked briefly at me. "Sorry."

She turned and started back inside her house. I followed. She stopped at the door and turned around. "I'd better get myself ready," she said. "Good-bye."

She softly shut her front door and I walked back to the Porsche. I sighed, thinking, "Jesus, these people and their luncheons. They're always having lunch." I started the car and roared away down the twisting, curving road. When I reached Sunset Boulevard, I turned right and headed for the ocean. It was another one of those beautiful California mornings. The only thing missing was Janet.

Ria and I drew closer and closer. I came to be a regular visitor at her home evenings after work and on weekends. She invited me for dinner often, and I learned that, unlike most of her wealthy friends, she really did most of the cooking herself. In a kitchen bigger than my entire Malibu apartment, she would throw a yeoman's apron over an elegant dinner dress and, armed with a vodka on the rocks, proceed, amid bursts of singing and near continuous chatter with Ella, to conjure up magnificent repasts.

An entire wall of the kitchen was designed for food storage. Floor-to-ceiling cabinets were jammed with supplies. There were two refrigerators and two 30-cubic-foot freezers. When I questioned Ria about maintaining this built-in cornucopia, I found that while she was aware of places like supermarkets, she never used them except in dire emergencies. All canned and bottled items were purchased by the case and delivered to her door. Also delivered to the servants' entrance were "cuts"—not slices—of meat, as well as fresh seafood and, as the occasion demanded, iced tins of gray beluga caviar. Eggs and milk were delivered daily. Vegetables and fruits came in an awninged pickup truck, which parked outside and waited for her to come out and make the various selections.

I had never seen strawberries the size of large plums. I had never known the gastronomical ecstasy of aged, prime steaks, perfectly marbled and so tender that chewing was almost optional.

I shook my head in delighted disbelief at all of this. Money, I decided, had more advantages than I had ever realized.

During these times—it was now May 1973—Ria and I usually dined alone. One evening in mid-May, after dining out, I joined Ria for what was now our customary afterdinner drink in the library.

"You know, Jim," she said, "things have been happening so fast since we've been together that I really haven't heard a word from you about what your life was all about before you met me."

She was sitting in her big, stuffed chair. Soft music was playing over the house's intercom. She regarded me with a curious smile. "Well?"

I got up from her desk chair where I was sitting and walked over to the fireplace. A small pile of wood had been stacked on the andirons with kindling beneath it. "Okay if I light the fire?" I asked.

"Sure," she said.

I lit one of the long fireplace matches and poked it under the kindling. Soon red-orange flames licked over the logs, and I stared into them. In the seven months since I had met this woman who was my mother, I had often verged on asking her about the circumstances of my birth, to tell me what she'd meant, that first day at the restaurant on La Cienega, when she spoke of what my father had done. I wanted to know, and I desperately did not want to know. If something ugly had happened, back there in Old Pine, and if I forced her to speak of it, a chill might settle upon our relationship, spoiling my nice new life. I wanted this nice new life, I was starved for it—not just the luxury and status but Ria's love. She had never volunteered to tell me more and, though I sometimes felt impelled to, I never inquired. Now, however, she had abruptly asked me about the past. What was she up to? A cold, sober wind of consciousness blew through me.

"Are you all right, Jim?"

I turned, looking across the room at her sitting in that chair.

"I'm okay," I said. "I guess I just . . ." I paused, biting my lower lip against a feeling that was building inside me. I was trying very hard to look at her as though she were just a friend, a woman I knew and liked a great deal. For some reason, I was trying very hard not to look at her as my mother.

"Dear," she said, concern showing in her eyes and voice, "I hope I haven't upset you. . . ."

"No, no, Ria," I interrupted, finally getting a grip on that feeling inside me. "No," I said, managing a smile, "that . . . that's all right. I've been wanting to tell you all along, I guess, but I think maybe I've been having such a good time with you that I sort of shoved everything way back in my mind."

I looked back into the flames of the fireplace.

"Well, maybe we should save this for another time, Jim," she said, getting up from her chair and walking over to where I stood. She touched her fingers to my face, turning me so that we were both looking each other in the eye. Looking into her eyes was like looking into my own. Without her ever saying so, I knew that she wanted very much to know about my childhood, but at the same time dreaded what she might hear. I put an arm around her and guided her back across the room to her chair. She sat down and I sat on the floor in front of her and began an edited recitation of my past. I kept it as light and cheerful as I could. I talked for almost two hours, until I was satisfied that she seemed satisfied. At the end, she said, "Now, that wasn't so hard, was it?"

I shook my head, smiling.

"Well, Jim," she said, "perhaps it's just as well that things turned out for us the way they did. You are a self-made man and, honey, I can tell you there aren't many of those your age in this neighborhood. If I had been able to keep you, and you had grown up here, it probably would have emasculated you."

I didn't say anything to that. I just smiled again and shrugged my shoulders. When Ria walked me to the door a short time later, I hardly heard the words she was saying. However calm I seemed, I was feeling fiercely that it was *not* just as well that things had turned out as they had. There was so much I had not told her.

•

# Chapter 5

As far as I knew, I was born July 12, 1940, in Stewart, West Virginia, the only son of Royce Hunter and Edith Cook Stingley, residents of Old Pine, North Carolina. How I came to be born in West Virginia, rather than North Carolina, was a funny family story. My mother, a secretary, was also an antique collector of no small dedication. So obsessed with this avocation was she, or so the story went, that in her ninth month of pregnancy she struck out from Old Pine in her Model A Ford, hot on the trail of some rare colonial item and quite forgetting that I was due very soon to make my entrance into the world. As she approached the city limits of Stewart, where the rare colonial item was for sale, I reminded her of the matter. She sought out the hospital and thus I arrived, all nine pounds, ten ounces. Seven days later she returned to Old Pine with me *and* the antique, she being a woman of unbending determination.

This story was told throughout my later childhood in Meadowbrooke to amuse visiting friends of the family. Some who heard it marveled that a woman of my mother's build—five feet tall and less than a hundred pounds—could produce a baby of such size. This was attributed to the genes of my father, a man who was nearly six feet tall and stocky. I eventually told the story myself, to friends or teachers who asked where I was born. I told it through and beyond my teen-age years, even when I had surpassed six feet two inches in height and weighed 245 pounds. I always did enjoy telling good stories.

The other story my parents liked to tell—this one presumably true—was how I won a beauty contest. I was a baby, in Old Pine, where my father worked for the U.S. Forest Service and my mother worked as a secretary. During the day I, like a lot of other children, was left in the care of a "colored girl." Sometimes, on warm summer days, these nursemaids would gather with their charges at a certain place along the causeway of the Owl River. To pass the time one day they held a baby beauty contest and I, with my head full of red curly hair, was declared the winner. My parents loved that story, but as I grew to be a teen-ager, I hated it. I knew boys were not supposed to win beauty contests, and, as a young teen-ager dealing with all the new manifestations and mysteries of maleness, this story did not help my shaky self-image. Even though I was as big as or bigger than any of my friends, I was passive, noncompetitive, and totally trusting—not the stuff of neighborhood heroes.

Whenever this story was told, or retold, at family gatherings, one of the listeners was sure to say, "Yes, I surely remember that. And, Jimmy, you know, you look just like your father." My father was virtually bald, and what hair he had was dark brown. My mother was dark, too, but no one ever claimed I resembled her. I looked for resemblance myself, but I never could find any. My sense of separateness was reinforced every summer at a yearly reunion of my mother's side of the family. There would be as many as a hundred people there and many of them, I was told, were my cousins. But I never felt any sense of kinship or belonging. They were all dark-haired, dark-complected people, small-boned and average to below average in height. There was not one physical similarity between myself and them.

I had no brothers or sisters, so until I was a teen-ager I spent most days with either a maid or my mother. My father was usually away, either working or fishing, so I can barely remember spending any time with both of them together, even on weekends. On holidays and during her vacations I would travel with my mother as she moved from Georgia to West Virginia in search of antiques. I would sit and stare out the car window while my mother spent an hour or so in each shop we visited.

She and I didn't talk much on the road. There was more talking at home, but always it was she who did the speaking. One thing she often spoke about was how little attention I paid to her directions and commands. What she didn't understand was that I barely heard her. I learned to read young, and in reading, found that I could escape to amazing worlds, simply by opening a book and turning the pages. My parents encouraged me, but the result was that I took things a step farther. My mind became a book. And when I wasn't actually reading, I was dreaming, lost in happy, exciting, and beautiful worlds where I wasn't lonely.

Increasingly exasperated, my mother took to corporal punishment as a way of getting my attention. Switches cut from a backyard tree and applied to the backs of my bare legs established very early on that she was an authority to be reckoned with. Unfortunately, the whippings did not have the effect she wanted. I sought respite in my daydreams all the more readily.

What my father thought of her methods, I don't know. These were the war years, and my father's job with the Forest Service was to put out fires caused by German submarines shelling the heavily wooded coast of North Carolina. Often he was away for days at a time, only to return exhausted, covered with soot from head to toe. To relax, he would go fishing and, upon his return, would regale his wide-eyed son with the heroic tall tales of his spectacular catches. For a solid German-American descended from Arkansas Baptists, my father, it now seems to me, was very Irish in his telling of fishing feats.

My mother was uninterested in his tales, but found a good use for the fish. Often she would take my father's rather large catch and distribute it among various poor black and white neighbors, all of whom, it would turn out, owned some antique or or other that my mother was interested in acquiring—at a bargain price, of course. When I grew old enough to understand what the word meant, she took some pride in describing herself to me as "penurious."

Penurious she was. When she spent money, even if it was for clothes, she called it an investment. When my father spent money, she called it a waste. She controlled the household purse, as I discovered when I became old enough to attend the Saturday double feature at the theater downtown. Each week she would give me exactly enough money to buy a ticket and either popcorn or a soda, never both.

My mother observed her own dictums. "You must not be extravagant," she told me, and she was not. On Christmas I would find under the tree shoes that never fit and clothes from the bargain store; birthdays were not occasions for presents of any kind. If I seemed disappointed she would say, "Now, Jimmy, you just have to be practical. We can't afford to waste money on things that are not practical."

In this fashion, I learned to expect little, and so, when my father decided I was old enough to come fishing with him, I was even more excited than most boys would have been. Away from home we formed a private, pleasurable bond. He would spend what seemed enormous sums of money on such items as Vienna sausages, hoop cheese, and crackers, with plenty of Pepsi to wash it all down. I learned to catch bluegills and catfish with my new cane pole. Eventually I graduated to the casting rod and, finally, the flyrod, all under the patient and caring tutelage of my father, who minimized my failures and lauded my accomplishments.

When we returned home he would fall silent in the presence of my mother. And she would have no ear for my excited versions of where we had been and what we had done. Instead, I would be told to "clean yourself up and don't make a mess of it. And when you're done with that, go to your room and clean it up. I've never seen anybody so sloppy and lazy in my life." And to my father she likely would say, "Well, how much trash did you fill his belly with?"

I would go to my room. I would hear them talking. Sometimes

the talk became heated and loud with anger and argument. I did not understand, but "money" and "liquor" and "women" and "spoiling that boy" seemed always to be the issues. Sometimes the word "divorce" came through the wall.

We had moved to Meadowbrooke, North Carolina, by then, and he had taken a job managing a nearby state forest. He abruptly left that job, became a private forestry consultant, and started drinking heavily. There were more fights at home. At first nothing changed between him and me. Our relationship was unaffected. But one day it was nearly destroyed. He had been "up the river," trolling for striped bass, and had returned home victorious with a 25-pound striper, the largest that had ever been caught in the Tar River. With me tagging along, he drove away from the house and hit bar after bar, showing off his catch and liberally toasting his accomplishment.

My mother had drilled into me that drunkenness was shameful, and this had been heavily reinforced by my Southern Baptist Sunday school. But I had never seen my father drunk. He had often come home "high," as it was put in those days, but this day I was to see him pie-faced. With each succeeding bar, he talked louder and louder. He began to stagger. I stood beside him, struggling to hold the heavy fish and blinking back tears of shame because people were laughing at him. Almost falling several times, he made his way out of the last bar and, with no little effort, to the car. I walked behind him, carrying the fish.

I opened the trunk of the car and laid the great creature on the spread of newspaper. As I closed the trunk I looked over to where my father ought to have been. He wasn't there. I walked around the car but he was nowhere in sight. I found him back in the bar, drinking another beer, with a pint whiskey bottle sticking out of his back pocket. Mustering all the nerve I had, I walked straight to him and tugged at his sleeve. "Daddy, can't we go home now? Please."

His hat was pushed back on his head. Sweat beaded on his forehead. He looked down at me. "Hey, son, where's the fish?" he said, slurring. "Gotta show these people that fish, boy. Biggest goddamn striper ever caught up that river."

"Daddy," I said "you've already shown 'em the fish. I put it back in the car. Please let's go home."

He raised his glass, a third of the beer running out of the corners of his mouth and down the front of his shirt. His eyes, usually soft hazel, looked glazed and sightless.

"Mister," urged the bartender, "you had better go on home now. We're about to close it down here."

My father, too drunk to know it was only nine o'clock, pulled his hat down over his eyes and staggered again toward the car. I took hold of his arm when we reached outside, and he shoved me down in the parking lot gravel. "Leave me alone," he muttered, fumbling for the keys.

I began crying then. "Daddy, let me drive. I can get us home. You've been drinking too much and I'm afraid. . . ."

He glared at me. "Get off the ground, boy," he barked. "And don't you tell me I can't drive, you little bastard."

He got in on his side of the car and I crawled in on mine. He tried three times to get the key in the ignition before he finallly succeeded. He started the car, stepping hard on the accelerator, making the engine roar. Jerking the car into reverse, he screeched backward, then jammed it into first gear and roared onto the highway.

"Daddy, you better turn on the lights," I said.

"Shut up, you smart aleck little bastard," he yelled, reaching, fumbling, and finally pulling the headlight switch on. "You don't know a goddamn thing. I'm driving this car and don't tell me I can't drive this car because I can! You hear?"

"Yes, Daddy," I said as we weaved from one side of the road to the other. I kept quiet then, and he stopped yelling. He gripped the steering wheel with both hands, and somehow, weaving all over the roads, we made it to the house. When he stopped the car, I opened the door and ran inside to my room and locked the door. I lay down on my bed, tears streaming into my pillow. Inside me was a hurt that seemed to grow bigger with every breath I took.

The next day at breakfast, my father sat at the table moaning theatrically, drinking Alka-Seltzer and trying to make a joke of

66

his hangover. I ate my breakfast in silence, gathered my school books, and walked out the door. I remember wondering: *If I cut my father with a knife . . . would he bleed?*

Something happened to me at that point. I began eating more and more, and getting fat. Pretty soon the kids at school were singing "Fatty, fatty, two-by-four, can't get in the kitchen door" whenever I appeared. That hurt, but food was an even better escape than reading or the Saturday matinee, so I kept on eating.

When I was thirteen my parents built a new house on the banks of Carver Bay. I was allowed in the den and the kitchen, but forbidden even to walk through the dining room or the living room where my mother displayed her antiques and held her bridge parties. She seemed to live in fear of me damaging or dirtying something valuable. Once, when I was helping her wash and dry some venerable bowls that were to be used at her bridge party that evening, I dropped one, and it shattered. It was the first time in my life I ever saw her cry.

"How could you! How could you be so—so . . . damned careless!" she said, kneeling beside the precious shards.

"Mama, Mama," I said, "I didn't mean to. I swear I didn't mean to, Mama. It just slipped."

She looked up at me, dark eyes and cold tears. Horrified at my deed, I begged her to let me repair it. "I can get some glue and fix it. Please, Mama!"

"Get out of this kitchen now," she said. Slowly, reverently, she was picking up the broken pieces. "Just get out of my sight."

Staying out of her sight became my vocation. Being in her sight meant new chores or criticisms. I never did well in school, I wasn't neat, and I did not have any school friends who met her standards. So, if I was in her sight, she railed.

"I just do not understand you, Jimmy. You have brains but you will not use them," she said every time I handed her my report card.

"Mama, I do too try," I would counter. "But I just don't understand things like arithmetic."

"You do *not* try! You are lazy and sloppy, and you just don't care how you make me look. Why, Jimmy? Why cannot you be like the rest of our friends' children? All of them make very good grades. All of them dress neatly and care about the way they look. And they do their chores without being told. But you, you don't try, Jimmy! You are an embarrassment to me. As hard as I have worked to give you every opportunity . . . and you do nothing. Why?"

I had no answer. I did not know then that I was the kind of person who had to be shown why something should or should not be done. I would only learn this about myself when I embarked on my career in journalism, where such a trait was considered valuable. I was a boy who questioned everything, and she was a woman who expected children always to do as they were told without asking questions. And because she never did anything but "tell" me what to do, I never did much of anything she said, unless I was physically forced.

As I grew older, I became warier. By the eleventh grade I had taken to staying out evenings—sweeping up somewhere, keeping score at basketball games—anything to stay away, particularly when Dad was home. I knew enough to realize when he would be at his drunkest, when the fighting would be at its peak. So when I headed my bicycle home, I would pull up a hundred yards short of the house and wait. When the light in his bedroom went out, I would give myself fifteen minutes and then quietly make my way to the house and steal upstairs as softly as I could.

But in June I flunked eleventh grade, and that night my father waited up for me. "You just don't give a damn, do you, boy?" he said, following me up the stairs. "I keep telling your mother that you'll make it, that you'll do all right, and goddammit you turn right around and fail in a high school where a fucking idiot can pass. What in the *hell* is the matter with you?"

I watched him weave back and forth as he stood belligerently before me. I was three inches taller and forty pounds heavier. I was fat, but I was also strong from playing football for a few years and lifting weights during training. He kept yelling. He was enumerating my shortcomings, a list of which I too could recite by rote. The more he spoke, the angrier I became. When he finished there was a pause. I looked right at him. "I might be a failure," I said, "but at least I'm not a drunk."

His eyes widened. He staggered toward me, swaying so close that the smell of bourbon filled my nostrils. His voice quivered. "Shut up! Shut your goddamned mouth! You don't *ever* talk to me like that!"

He tried to grab me by the shirt. When he did, I hit him. He crumpled and fell to the floor at my feet. I stood there, tears running down my cheeks. Slowly he struggled back up, holding onto the bedpost. He did not look at me, but instead righted himself and, staggering, made his way to the stairs. I stood there numb and scared. I figured any second he would turn around, come back and beat the hell out of me for what I had done. But the downstairs door closed and did not reopen. I sat down on the bed. My fear was replaced with guilt, with shame, and with sadness.

The next year I flunked eleventh grade for the second time. Now I was eighteen and had to register for the draft. But when I went to the local board to register, I was told I had to have a birth certificate. Dad was working in Tennessee. I told my mother. "Oh," she said. "Well, Jimmy, I don't think we have your birth certificate here. I'll have to write to West Virginia for it. I'll do that right now."

When it came from West Virginia in the mail, she looked at it and handed it to me. She returned to the den, where she was reading. "Mama," I said, walking into the den. "This says I was born on June 26, 1940. I thought my birthday was July 12."

"It does?" she said, not lifting her eyes from her book. "Well, Jimmy, I guess we just got the dates mixed up."

"Oh," I said, examining the certificate. "Well, I guess I'm older than I thought I was, huh?"

"Well, it doesn't matter," she said, still looking down at her book. "Birthdays are not all that important anyway. You know that, Jimmy."

"Yes, Mama, I guess," I said.

"What's important," she said, looking up at me this time, "is your getting a high school diploma."

To that end, I was dispatched to a military academy in Virginia where for the next two years I lived in a world that was advertised as the perfect place to teach a young man the responsibilities of life. I flunked there too, the first year. But I was sent back. The second year I finally got the diploma, and in the fall of 1960 I entered a small teacher's college. I chose English as my major because I was reasonably certain I could pass it. Even in the eleventh grade, when I had failed every other course—twice —I had gotten A's in English. This had not impressed my mother, however. English came easy to me. My mother was suspicious of anything that came easy.

When I turned in the first English composition, the professor asked me to remain after class. "Jim," she said, holding the paper in her hands, "you have unusual talent. I'm going to ask a favor from you. I want you to go over to the college newspaper—I will call Dr. Rowe, the adviser there, and tell him you're coming— and I want you to write for the paper. Will you do that?" I said I would, and I thanked her, although I wasn't quite sure then for what. But as it turned out, I loved writing, loved seeing my name above my pieces, and soon was writing my own column.

Suddenly, I felt that I belonged to the human race. The feeling intoxicated me. I wanted to be a part of everything, because for so long I had been part of nothing. I pledged a fraternity, I joined the chorus, I offered my poetry to the campus magazine. I made dean's list.

When I returned home for the quarter break, I couldn't wait to talk to my father. Thinking he was in Tennessee, I asked my mother when Dad was going to be home.

"Jimmy," she said, "your father is in Bowman Gray Hospital in Winston-Salem. He had a sort of a . . . well, breakdown. He's being treated for hypertension."

"Can I go see him?"

"No, Jimmy. It's best you don't."

That was all that was said of it, but the part that was left unsaid bothered me deeply. I suspected something was seriously wrong with my father. Back at school, I retreated to my office at the paper. I wrote reams and reams of copy, but didn't save any energy for my classes. At the end of the quarter, I was told I had to leave the campus. I had failed every single course.

I turned twenty-one in June 1961. My father was out of the hospital and doing consulting work in Tennessee. I was living at home and working as a patrolman with the Meadowbrooke Police Department. In terms of social status, policemen ranked just below cab drivers and just above "pulpwood niggers" from the local paper mills. When news of my new job got out, I could almost hear the gasps of my mother's friends. The silence from my mother loudened.

In February of 1962, my mother was visiting relatives across the state, and my father returned from Tennessee. It was the first I had seen him in a long time. He was no longer drinking. He was as he had been in the old days, when we had been so close. He was looking much better, and his mood was lighter. He and I sat and talked late into the night. I had been losing weight, and I told him I had applied to the U.S. Air Force and it looked as if I might be accepted.

"That might be real good for you, son," he said. "Hell, you'd get a chance to travel around the world and see things that you might not otherwise ever get a chance to see. It might give you some perspective too. I've always felt inside me that you're going to be real special in some way, son. It's just taking some time for you to get there. But you will. I know you will."

I loved my father that night. He finally had told me what I craved to hear. He didn't see me as a disgrace because I was a cop. He saw me only as his son, his son whom he loved, his son whom he wanted only happiness for. We said good night and I fell asleep feeling for the first time in so many years that at last my father and I were going to be the friends that we had always wanted to be.

The next morning I went to work at 7:00 A.M. When I got home in the late afternoon there was a note on the kitchen counter. "Son—Have gone up the river to see what I can do to the bass population and maybe even knock down a mallard or two. There's some baloney and cheese in the refrigerator for you. I'll see you a little after dusk. It was good talking with you last night. Love, Dad."

He had written the note on the back of an eight-by-twelve photo of me in a cop's uniform. In the picture I was trying to look tough. I changed from my uniform into jeans and a shirt and looked around the house. Uncharacteristically, I began sweeping the floors and dusting the furniture, and finally attacked the kitchen and its pile of dirty dishes.

By 5:00 P.M. I had finished. I was standing at the sink, looking out as the winter darkness began closing in, when an emptiness slowly, steadily began making itself felt inside me. I looked at the clock and it was 5:30. Tears began forming in my eyes. Suddenly a voice without substance, without sound, told me my father was dead. I walked into the den and looked out across the bay. All that was left to see now was the flat, gray outline of the bay's expanse. "He's not coming back, son," the same soundless voice said. "He's not coming back."

What I did then is a blur to me. I remember driving straight to City Hall where my dad's best friend, Taft Buckner, was attending a City Council meeting. I told him only that I was very worried about Dad. It was past dark and he hadn't returned.

At first Taft tried to reassure me, but I insisted.

"No, Taft," I said. "Something's wrong. I just feel it. I just know it."

He looked at me for a moment, and he knew I was very serious and very upset. Together we went to the police and called out the rescue squad to search the upper river for my father. I went out with the squad myself. I rode in the lead boat because I was familiar with my father's fishing grounds. We went up river seven miles, to my father's favorite spot, but there was nothing in sight. Then I remembered another spot, several miles farther up, and we headed there.

But when we approached a certain bend, I held up my hand to stop the boat. "He wouldn't be any farther up than this," I lied. "Let's turn around and go down river. Maybe he went out on the bigger water to try for some ducks." We turned around and started back in the other direction. I looked over my shoulder at that dark bend. I knew he was there. I knew he was dead. I could not bring myself to see him dead. I had to remember him alive.

Thirty minutes after dawn they found him. The coroner told me that the outboard motor must have caught fire and when my father turned around to smother the flames with a tarpaulin, he had suffered a massive heart attack that killed him instantly. "It happened real fast," I was told. "He didn't suffer. It hit him so quick, his glasses were still on his head when they found him." The coroner placed the time of death at between 5:00 and 6:00 P.M. the day before.

I called my mother. "Yes, Jimmy, what is it?" she asked when she was brought to the phone.

I tried to get a grip on myself. I tried hard not to cry. I did not succeed.

"Jimmy," she said, "what in the world is wrong?"

"Mama," I finally managed to say, "Daddy's dead."

There was a short pause, and she began crying. She never questioned what I had said. The way I had said it left no doubt. The police chief took the phone, and I sat down on the couch, not hearing anymore, not feeling, not seeing, as he supplied the details.

After my father died I moved to an attic apartment across town. I took with me two of his possessions: his hand-crafted cypress fishing tackle box and an ashtray. The ashtray had a copper base, from which a twisting bronze sailfish rose into the air. It was a fish my father had always wanted to catch and never did.

What little taste I had for police work left me. I thought again of joining the military. Then a friend who was a reporter urged me to write articles for the local newspaper. It was like writing in college, only much better because this was a newspaper that people paid to read. When I was offered the job of full-time reporter, I happily turned in my shield and my .357 Magnum.

My mother seemed pleased about this new job, but she seemed to view the whole thing as a fluke. She assumed I would eventually return to college and get a teaching job, a more practical way of earning a living.

Then something occurred that drove us even further apart: I got a raise. It was only five dollars a week. But to me it signified the beginning of a real future. After years of being an embarrassment, I felt like a pillar of the community, and I did what I thought was the right thing. I bought a new car, new furniture, and new clothes. I even bought a house. I bought most of it on credit, from merchants who knew my family was a good risk. That I was one Stingley who was *not* a good risk soon became very apparent. Overnight, I had more payments per month than salary. When I couldn't ignore the problem any longer, I went to my mother and asked for a loan of two thousand dollars, explaining my situation.

"How could you?" she asked. "How could you embarrass me like this? How many times have I told you not to borrow money, not to use credit? How many times have I told you, Jimmy, that you must be practical? That you must save your money before you can have anything? But no, oh, no. You never listen to me. Well, you can stew in your own juice. I am not about to give you any money. Not a penny. If you're not going to listen to me, then you'll just have to learn the hard way." The next week my furniture, house, and car were repossessed. The people who did it were nice about it. They didn't threaten or press me for the money they had lost. They were very understanding.

Clearly, I needed a change of scene. In due course I got a job offer from a larger paper, but I was afraid to take it—afraid I would fail. I turned to a good friend, John Boitnott, whom I had met back on the police force. He was a World War II veteran with a lifetime's worth of wisdom and experience. "Son," he told me, "I have tried mightily not to preach to you, but I want you to trust me on this. Because I'm telling you this for the very simple reason that I know who you are. You don't know who you are. You will, some day, but for right now, just listen and do. Take that job. And take the job that comes after it. Never be afraid of taking a chance at bettering yourself. The thing is, Jim, think of it this way. Think of yourself twenty years down the road and the fact that you never did take that chance. You'll wonder what it would have led to. Better you find out, son. Better you find out, always."

And so I began. Over the next eight years I went from one paper to the next, always taking a shot at the next biggest thing up the line. And it worked. Professionally I was on my way to the top and I wasn't going to quit until I got there. And I kept getting there. I reported for the *Raleigh-News & Observer*, then joined United Press International in Boston. The loneliness of that big, northern city did not suit me. One day I went to Logan International Airport and caught the first plane flying south. Three months later I had landed a job at the *Fort Lauderdale News*. Five months later I drew my first Pulitzer Prize nomination.

Since becoming a journalist I had talked to my mother rarely, and always long distance. When I was nominated for the Pulitzer, I returned home but not to share my accomplishment with her. I borrowed her car and drove several miles west to the cemetery where my father was buried. It had been seven years since I had been to his grave, but in my mind I knew exactly where it was. I parked the car and got out, walking straight across the hundreds of flat bronze plaques that dotted the vast lawn until I came to a tall longleaf pine. It was there, I remembered, that he lay. But when I reached the pine, his grave was not to be found. I searched the bronze plaques again, bewildered. The tree had been imbedded in my memory all those years. Finally I started making wider and wider circles around the tree until at last, far from the pine, I saw the plaque spelling out his name.

I went to his grave and stood there. After a few minutes I knelt down. "Daddy . . ." I began crying. "I'm sorry, Daddy," I said. "I'm so sorry you couldn't be here now. I finally did it, Daddy. I finally made it . . . just like you said I would. I finally made it!"

In July 1968, I found myself being courted by a number of larger newspapers. This was not exactly serendipity, since after the Pulitzer nomination I had hit the road and marketed myself vigorously. My salesmanship had paid off. The highest bidder turned out to be the *San Diego Union*. They flew me to San Diego, put me up in the Grant Hotel, filled my pockets with Yellow Cab ticket books, and paid my way for a week while I toured the area to decide if the paper was the right choice. It was heady stuff for me, so heady that I never seriously examined the paper and what it stood for.

I made the move to San Diego in September. I wrote stories about the Chicanos and Black Panthers, movements in the city that seriously intended to challenge the status quo. Some stories never ran. Those that did run were so heavily edited I barely recognized them. One editor of the *Union,* a kindly man whose weary eyes met mine over the rims of his half-glasses, summed it up one night when I turned in another story that would never see the light of day. "Jim," he said, "it's very sad that you are working here. Very sad."

I knew my tenure at the *Union* would not be a long one. In the meantime I worked off my frustrations in a physical fitness program that included about three hours of body surfing each day at a small beach in La Jolla, and a rigorous bicycle routine. Soon I was in better condition than I had ever been in my life. No longer was there an ounce of fat. I weighed in at 197 pounds, had a 31-inch waist and a 46-inch chest. I had lost 63 pounds.

But there was one frustration that nothing would not ease. Without consulting me, my mother had begun to sell off the family's land holdings. First, she disposed of nearly one hundred acres of timberland. It was. land that I cherished, land I had walked with my father many times. The ridges and swamps were a haven for me, and I had always assumed it would be mine to walk upon. Next she sold a beautiful piece of acreage in the Blue Ridge Mountains. Again, she did so without telling me beforehand, never even offering me the first chance to buy. I would learn what had happened during a phone call or a visit home; she would mention the sale matter-of-factly, as if I had only a slight passing interest. If I questioned her, she would stiffen and only say she needed the income, that her retirement income was insufficient. She never explained why she never offered me first refusal

76

on my father's property. She seemed affronted that I challenged her at all.

So I did not question her again. It was another door shut between us, another edict declaring that I was no part of her. Her control was total. It always had been total. Lying alone in my bed in San Diego, I unknowingly made a vow. I would never beg women. I would never be in their debt.

By August 1969 I had been at the *Union* for almost a year. I had given up trying to be a reformer and had chosen assignments I knew would conform to the paper's notions of acceptability; I'd needed to get stories printed to add depth to my portfolio. And I'd needed to put some energy into my off-duty hours. During that year I had begun to allow women to enter my life—although only on my terms. It wasn't so difficult. This was the Age of Aquarius in Southern California. It was a perfect time and place for someone—and there were many of us—who wanted no commitments. The women I chose at first were sweet and, above all, submissive. I was new to the game but I soon learned to play it for my pleasure. When the pleasure wore thin, the women no longer existed. Some cried and wanted to know what was the matter. "I just don't want to see you anymore," I'd say. I would feel guilty, but only until I found a body to replace the one I'd just disposed of.

After that one year at the *Union* it was time to get moving again. Los Angeles was only 120 miles north, and I was ready to make my play for the big time. I had read the *Los Angeles Times* every day for a year, studying its format, envying its quality and range. The *Times* was the largest standard-size newspaper in the United States. Its circulation was then about 1.3 million daily and it employed a staff of journalists who were not just the best in the West, but among the best in the world. They produced fine writing, the kind that took a lot of time, money, and energy, the kind I was starving to do. Just as important, from where I stood, the *Times* seemed to know no bounds, to have no fears about reporting what was really happening late in the explosive sixties.

I placed a call to the *Times*'s managing editor, Frank Haven.

Haven referred me to metropolitan editor William F. Thomas, who rather hurriedly informed me that he got 200 applications a month from journalists all over the world and, besides, there wasn't an opening. I told him I just wanted him to do one thing—read some of my clips. There was a pause. "Okay," he said, apparently amused by the determination in my voice. "Bring them up here next, uh—Wednesday. I've got time to see you then."

When I arrived the next Wednesday, Thomas was nowhere to be found. I left the package of clips with Jack Goulding, the day city editor, who said he would see that they reached Thomas. In two weeks I received a call from Thomas. He said they still didn't have an opening on the metropolitan staff, but asked if I would consider a zone edition assignment until an opening came up. What he was asking me to do was cover strictly local news in one of Los Angeles's innumerable suburbs.

"How long are you talking about?" I asked.

"Three months," he said.

"When can I start?" I asked.

"Give 'em your notice," he said. "We'll see you in two weeks."

I hung up the phone, and sat there in the city room of the *Union* for a few minutes, smoking a cigarette and feeling a beautiful warm sensation that was coursing through me like a relentless orgasmic comet. The friendly editor looked over at me, his sad eyes, as always, peering over the tops of his glasses. "Watcha got today, Jim?" he asked. I smiled at him, put a piece of paper in my typewriter, and wrote my resignation.

On September 22, 1969, I reported to Bill Thomas and began my career with the *Times*. After the three-month zone period, I was brought into the metropolitan room. Thanks to Thomas, my freedom seemed unlimited. If I couldn't come up with a good story idea, he'd come up with one for me. I spent most of my time on the road or in the air, covering such events as the Attica prison riot, the burning of the Bank of America, and the subsequent student riots at the University of California–Santa Barbara. I chased Howard Hughes down to the Bahamas and even spent a weekend with Sonny Barger and his Hell's Angels at their annual Labor Day orgy on the shores of Madeira County's Bass Lake.

I turned thirty the following June. A few weeks later I was doing my laundry in the basement of my apartment building when Theresa came in and asked if my machine would be free soon. We began to see each other, and it seemed as if everything was falling into place. I had grown up and made good in all the important ways but one. Marriage and a family seemed the natural, inevitable next step. And I knew it would make Mama happy.

We flew to Meadowbrooke for the wedding and my old paper, the *Pilot News,* ran an editorial to welcome me: "A native son returned briefly to Meadowbrooke today. Jim Stingley came home. Stingley will be married here Saturday and then he returns to a challenging newspaper role that has carried him thousands of miles across the length and breadth of America. . . ." If anybody at the *Times* had ever seen that article, I'd have been hoo-hawed for months. Still, it was my town, and I couldn't help feeling elation mixed with pride.

Now, I thought, my mother and I would finally be close. Now I had done everything she could want me to do. I was, as the editorial went on to say, "a standout newspaperman" with "a fine career." And I was getting married to a sweet young woman. The wedding reception was held at my mother's house. I was standing in the reception line, and my mother was standing just a few feet away, talking to an old friend of hers. "You just don't know how hard this has been on me," she said, "hosting Jimmy's wedding. I mean, that's usually the job of the bride's parents. I just don't understand why he didn't have the wedding in California and bring me out there. It certainly would have made things much easier on me. I'm not a spring chicken, you know."

Back in Los Angeles, Theresa and I leased the house in the Valley.

Then, Ria Dammeron's letter arrived.

Chapter 6

"Did you ever know?"

I was almost asleep when she asked the question. We had spent the evening at Trader Vic's, feasting on spareribs, egg rolls, and shrimp. Now we were in Ria's library, and I was stretched out on the couch, drowsy and satisfied.

Ria had changed into a powder-blue dressing gown and was sitting in the corner of the couch, with one leg curled up under her and the fingers of her left hand stroking the curls of my hair.

"About you?" I asked. "No."

"They never told you about me?"

"No. Oh, there were some hints, some clues. But I only understand them now, in retrospect."

"What sort of clues?"

I laughed. "It's kind of funny, actually. You see, my mother never acknowledged my birthday. I mean, there was never a real thing made over it—no cakes, candles, presents, or parties. It was just that every year, on July 12, I became older."

"July 12?"

"That was what my mother told me. I didn't know my real

birthday until I was old enough to go into the army." Then I told her the story of the date discrepancy on my birth certificate and how my mother dismissed the matter as something unimportant. Ria was silent. Her fingers stopped moving through my hair.

"What's wrong?" I asked.

"Jim, you weren't born on June 26, either."

I smiled painfully, letting out a long sigh. "I wonder," I said, looking into her eyes, "how much more of me there isn't."

"Or is?" she said. "Listen, darling, I want to tell you the whole story. But . . . well, not tonight. Not here. I don't want to have any interruptions. Let's meet at your place this weekend . . . say, Saturday afternoon?"

She kissed me softly, full on the lips. I kissed her back. She moved her lips away from mine and we hugged for a long moment, her cheek next to mine. I felt her tears on my face.

Then she drew back her head and managed a little grin.

"The story, you know, does have a happy ending," she said.

My eyes were full of her. "I hope so," I said. "I sure hope so."

As I looked at her, I felt as I had that first day we met in the restaurant. Again we were blending, merging, and I felt a complicated mix of emotions course through me. I wanted to hold her. I wanted her to hold me.

I shook those thoughts and feelings away. They came back. I shook them away again. They returned. I looked at Ria and I could have sworn she knew exactly what I was feeling. She said nothing. She just kept looking me in the eyes.

I sat up and rubbed my face with my hands.

"Tired?" she said.

"Yeah. Tired and sleepy," I said, lighting a cigarette.

"Do you want to spend the night here? There's plenty of space, now that I'm living alone."

I looked at her. She was leaning back into the corner of the couch, studying me with a scrutiny that was both exciting and unsettling.

"Well?" she said.

I let out a long sigh, shaking my head. "I'd better get on back

81

out to Malibu," I said. "I've got an early morning interview." I felt she knew that was a lie.

The morning fog had just burned off the Malibu waves when she arrived at my apartment that Saturday. Surfers, like human seals in their black wet suits, dotted the waters behind the wave line, waiting their endless wait. The Pacific Coast Highway was crammed with cars and vans, full of people ready to hit the beach. I met Ria outside as she, dressed in slacks, blouse, and high heels, came cautiously up the steps with bags from her Beverly Hills grocer cradled in each arm.

"I brought a little lunch," she said, and then kissed me. "I was thinking this might be a long session, and I don't want to interrupt it by having to go somewhere to eat."

I took the bags from her and led her up the steps. In the kitchen I unpacked Ria's "little lunch," a gourmet's gold mine of smoked salmon, caviar, white wine, and Brie. It was the sort of costly snack that I had become accustomed to. "Plebian fare," I said, "but I suppose we can improvise."

"Well," she said, "these are hard times, you know."

"Yeah." I sighed, squinting at the label on one of the tins. "Life's hell when you can only get beluga black."

We settled down on a couch facing the picture window. Beyond the highway and the beachhouses lay the blueness of the Pacific. Folding her hands into her lap, she stared silently at the carpet.

By now I had come to learn that this was a prelude. When Ria had something she deemed important to say, she always went silent first, like an actress going over her lines. She would get a sort of hazy, faraway look in her eyes. Finally, when she knew her audience was quiet and waiting, she would begin.

Ria cleared her throat. I settled back, lit a cigarette, and readied myself to spend however many hours it was going to take. This was one story I intended to listen to.

"I was a little girl when I met your mother and father," she began. "When I say little, I mean I was only sixteen years old. My body"—she smiled—"was, shall we say, quite a bit older,

82

more like the body of a very well-developed woman. Of course, I didn't know anything at all about such things then, but in retrospect I guess I looked like I knew.

"Anyway, I was really an innocent little girl. I had been born in a wood frame house in Mount Elgin, a rural community built on swampy ground not too far inland from Nag's Head, and I had never been anywhere except Lassiter, which was about two miles away, and Oakmount, another little town fifty miles away. The only reason I ever went to Oakmount was because my father lived there. You see, my mother died of malaria when I was two years old, and I was raised by my grandfather until I was seven."

She lifted her chin and closed her eyes. When she opened them again, it seemed as though her spirit had flown off someplace and returned sadly. "Grandpa Stafford," she went on, "was my mother, my father . . . everything to me. He was a big man and pretty tough, I guess. He owned a lumber mill and kept things going even though the Great Depression hit. But to me he was just gentle and sweet. He spoiled me rotten. He took me everywhere with him, let me play in the sawdust pile at the mill. At the general store he'd buy me a lemon and cut the top off it and put a peppermint stick in it."

Her voice wavered. "He died when I was seven years old. I never will get over the grief of losing him. It was like losing my whole world. I remember him laid out in death under a huge oak tree. My cousins were playing Ring-around-the-rosie around his casket. I was absolutely furious at them. How could they play games while my grandpa was lying there dead?" She went silent again, staring at her lap.

"What happened to your father?" I finally said. "Why didn't he take care of you?"

"Oh," she said softly, a wry smile crossing her face, "Big Red wasn't much of a family man. He was known for his singing—he had a fabulous bass voice—and he was actually quite a wonderful man in so many ways. Very charming.

"But he was perhaps a bit allergic to work. I don't want to be unfair to him—it was the Depression and work was hard to come by—but he really preferred to play his fiddle at the Saturday night dances. That, or hunt and fish. Anyway, he farmed me out to kinfolk, and my two brothers, too. He got married again and took up residence in Oakmount. That's how I happened to visit there. After grandfather died, I lived with Uncle Eugene Covington and Aunt Hedy during the winter; then, summers I would go stay with my father.

"But those were pretty bad times. My stepmother was a mean, insane woman who twice tried to kill me. It got so bad that I ran away from my father's home after one of her attacks. After that I never went back to Oakmount again unless my stepmother was going to be away taking care of her sick mother. When she would return, I would leave and go back to Uncle Eugene's. But I really wasn't very happy there, either. While they always were nice to me, it really was just more of the same boring life. When I was in Oakmount, I cooked, cleaned, and took care of my father. When I was back in Mount Elgin, I was the cook and housekeeper for my aunt and uncle. It wasn't much fun getting up at four in the morning to cook breakfast for my uncle, then working all day scrubbing floors. And they didn't have a radio; there were no movies. The only real fun I had was singing at the Free Will Baptist Church.

"So," she said, "that was pretty much my life until I met your mother."

"You mean, the woman who raised me," I said, getting up to pour a glass of wine.

"Well, dear, she is your mother in the sense that legally she's your mother. Would you fix me a vodka?"

I tensed at her insistence on the technicality but didn't say anything. I returned and handed her what she'd ordered. "And you were sixteen then?" I asked, sitting back down beside her.

"Yes. I'd turned sixteen and was visiting my father in Oakmount that summer. I had been working all day cleaning the house and was lying on the sofa exhausted when the doorbell rang. This small woman was at the door. She had dark hair, was not terribly attractive to look at, was rather plain, in fact. But she seemed nice and she said she wanted to speak to either my mother or father about some antiques she was looking for.

"I told her no one but me was home right then. Instead of leaving, she stayed for two hours, just talking to me about the Victorian antiques she was looking for and generally just being very friendly. She returned the following day. Again, I was alone. This time she asked me if I was happy with my life there and if I had had any ideas about living elsewhere. Then she told me that she lived in a town called Old Pine, which I'd never heard of, that she was married to a forest ranger, and that she had an elderly mother who had a general store in another town somewhere. She stressed that her mother was physically afflicted and she was very concerned about finding someone to help care for the old lady and run the store. Then she asked me if I would ever consider taking such a job.

"Well, she sure made it sound appealing. I told her yes, I would consider it because, I told her, I was having great difficulties with my stepmother. So she gave me her address and left. A very short time later, I remember writing to her and telling her that my stepmother had returned, and was the job with her mother still open? I received a letter within the week saying yes and that she would come get me . . . which she did."

Ria sipped the last of her vodka and handed the glass to me. As I went to the kitchen to make her another drink, she continued speaking.

"Edith came for me. At first, my father was against the idea, but he knew how much I hated my stepmother and finally he said, well, if that's what you want, do it. So we left. And on the way Edith was delightful as she talked, planting great pictures in my mind about the lovely new life I was going to have—how it was going to be a very pleasant life, taking care of her mother, running the store, being able to be on my own for the first time.

"When we reached Old Pine, I was thrilled and impressed with everything I saw—the boats on the river, the beautiful little apartment Edith had that faced the river, her collection of shiny and fine antiques that were so well-preserved. And my room was perfect. It was little but charming, with chintz curtains. But it was not inside her apartment. It was located on the same floor, but outside the apartment. I didn't meet your father that first day. In fact, he didn't arrive for several days. But I remember, when he did arrive, how he was so attractive. He had a high, wide forehead; broad shoulders; and a virile, good-looking face. He was very pleasant to me. I remember we had supper together."

Ria smiled, shaking her head. "The next morning I woke up to find this same man in bed with me. It scared the holy bejesus out of me. I had never seen a man nude before and certainly had never seen an erection before. I was totally terrified. I froze."

"Did you scream for help?" I asked.

"Oh, God, no. I was too scared. But I think that scared him, because he got up and left. And I remember thinking, Good Lord, what am I going to say to my new friend, Edith? I was so embarrassed and ashamed."

"What did you say to her?" I asked.

"Nothing. Not the first time. You have to remember, Jim, I might have been stacked and looked twenty, but I had the innocence of a ten-year-old. But about a week later, he came in again. The same scenario followed. Nothing happened. But this time, after a day or so, I went to Edith and asked her if I couldn't please go where I was supposed to go and stay with her mother. And she gave me some sort of vague excuse, and the matter was sort of brushed aside.

"Well, then everything was very quiet and normal for a while. And the three of us would go—this was in June or July—to the beach. It was a long drive and we always carried a picnic of deviled eggs and such that Edith and I would prepare."

"What beach did you go to?" I asked.

"Oh, darling, I couldn't possibly remember that."

"Ria, did my father drink much on those trips?"

She looked at me with surprise. "Oh, dear no. Your father never drank the entire time I knew him. He . . ." Her voice trailed off. "He was really . . . a very bright, warm man." There was a pause. "Anyway, Edith really attended to me during those times. Once she took me out and bought me a very pretty black and white dress. We would spend days, she and I, just going around to antique shops and historical places around Old Pine. The odd thing was she kept putting me off about going to her mother's.

But it really didn't matter much to me by then because life was, for the first time, very pleasant for me. I didn't have any problems, I was never a slave in her home. In fact, I was just as happy as I could be. We did so many things together that soon I felt like I was her daughter."

Ria's tone of voice almost took the sound of a little girl's as she spoke now. "Edith taught me so many things and they were really exciting things for a backwoods girl who never finished the ninth grade. She told me her life story, about how she once worked in New York. In fact, that was the first time I had heard of New York and what an exciting city it was. We just had a wonderful time together."

Her eyes changed; she was Ria the woman again. She put down her drink, stood up, and walked across the room to the window. She looked out at the coast highway jammed with speeding cars. "Then late summer came," she said, "and one night the three of us were going to go to a movie, as we occasionally did. We had supper, were all dressed to go, when Edith suddenly said she was coming down with a migraine headache. I remember that she did suffer from headaches. Anyway, she told me, 'Oh, don't worry about me, you and Roy go to the movie.' It was chilly that night, so she got a coat of hers and gave it to me, saying 'The coat's short on you, but it will keep you warm. Enjoy the movie!' "

Ria turned from the window and came back to the couch, seating herself across from me again, picking up her drink again. She slowly took a long sip.

"So I went along with Roy—your father—to the movie," she finally said. "Only we didn't go to a movie. He drove the car to a deserted area in the woods where he overpowered me, undressed me, tore my panties off me, and had his way with me. He was such a strong man there was nothing I could do." Ria sighed, shaking her head dramatically. "I was in such pain, such agony from it. There was blood all over the car, all over the back seat. Then I sort of blacked out. When I came to, he had dressed me, and we were on the way home. I went to my room. I remember I could not walk without pain for a week."

As I listened to Ria's words, I was horrified by the image of my father doing that to her.

"Ria . . ."

"He had intercourse with me more than once. I was always cornered and overpowered, I certainly had no feelings of pleasure. Because every time it hurt. I sort of checked out while he was doing it. Because I felt trapped . . . and didn't know what else to do."

"But Ria, why didn't you tell Edith about it?"

"I was too ashamed, Jim. I was too embarrassed that my friend's husband had taken advantage of me. I didn't want to hurt Edith. She had been so good to me. Also, I had good feelings about your father—except during times like those.

"Anyway, it finally got to where I was afraid to stay in my room at night, because that's when he would come in on me. And finally I told Edith that I needed to go back home. She tried to make me stay, but she didn't insist. And, of course, she had no idea what was going on. Well, no sooner had I returned to my aunt and uncle's than I missed a period. I knew I was pregnant. And I was terrified. I didn't have any money, and I didn't really have a home. I certainly wouldn't have had a home if my aunt had known. The whole community would have come down on our entire family. Getting pregnant without being married was an absolute taboo. So I did the only thing I knew. I wrote to Edith and told her of my circumstance. She was very sympathetic and wrote back for me not to worry, she was my friend and she understood. She said she would come get me and I could live with her and Roy. So, she came and got me."

"Didn't she suspect anything?"

"No. She probably figured it was some boy back home. But she told me that in a way, it might have been a blessing in disguise. She said that she and Roy had never been able to have children and that maybe this would be a solution for all of us. That she would take care of me, and then when the baby came, they could adopt it. I didn't know what to say. I just knew I needed to be taken care of, and she was the only person who could do it."

I shook my head slowly. "Ria. How many times did my father, uh—corner you?"

"As few times as I could get by with. I do remember that it was always in the middle of the night, and there was always a struggle. I never went willingly. But I was intimidated by him. I—I seem to remember that he tried to kiss me."

"And you never screamed or cried out?"

"I was too terrified that Edith would hear, darling. Anyway, after Edith came for me, I was back living with them again. They moved to a home in the country outside of Old Pine, but it was still located near the river shore. Things were different then. I was more or less treated like a servant and kept hidden. The bed in my room was a homemade bed, made by your father out of wood frame and chicken wire, period. The story they told visitors was that I was Edith's niece and I was married to a serviceman. Your mother by now had told her friends she was pregnant and had begun to pad herself because I had started to show. She told me that this way her friends in Old Pine would think that the baby really was hers. I just went right along with her. But Edith was marvelous. It was always a mother-daughter routine between us. She said another reason she would take the baby was so that I would never have to suffer the shame of people knowing.

"Well, anyway, as the months passed, Edith finally moved me to a roominghouse in Richmond, Virginia. It was a nice room. She would leave me there, but she would never be gone more than three days. Again, the story was that I was her niece and all. Your father, posing as my uncle, came to visit . . . to verify to the landlady, I suppose, that I was married and my husband was in the service.

"I was very lonely there. There was a Victrola in the room and one record—the 'Merry Widow Waltz.' That and a few books were all I had to amuse me. I remember standing at my window and watching the streets below. There were a lot of young soldiers always walking by, and I remember thinking how sad it was that my life had to be the way it was, that I couldn't be out being the young girl that I should have been. All I did was play the

'Merry Widow Waltz.' " she laughed. "I was really quite fond of it."

I smiled back at her, but my heart was aching.

"Well, when I was almost ready to give birth, your mother moved us to Stewart, a town in West Virginia. She rented a coal miner's cabin with an outhouse. I remember the two of us made some lima bean soup one evening and then I got the damnedest bellyache I'd ever had in my life. And it was you. I remember"— she grimaced—"the ambulance came and I was put in it. I was in such agony, I thought surely I was going to die! God, such agony! Then I passed out. When I came to I was back in this coal miner's shack with your father beside me. It was just before my eighteenth birthday. I remember your father being so distraught because in giving birth to you, I had nearly died. I didn't dilate and they had to cut me to remove you. And then I started hemorrhaging. . . ."

Ria's voice stopped and she put her face in her hands. Her body began to shake. I could only watch her. Finally, she stopped shaking and lifted her head. Tears were in her eyes, and she wiped them away with her hands, smearing her mascara.

"Slowly," she went on, "I recuperated. After six or eight weeks, I was back on my feet again. During that whole time, Edith took care of you. She wouldn't even let me diaper you or breast feed you. I was still pretty sick. Then she sent me back home to my aunt. Well, then my life started all over again. When my mother had died she'd left me land that she'd inherited from *her* father. I asked my uncle to pay me for that land so I could pay my way through beauty school. I thought surely he would do that for me because the school didn't cost but about a hundred dollars." She frowned. "He paid me twenty-one dollars for my land and timber and then he loaned me the hundred dollars, which I never paid back because he stole that land from me and my brothers.

"Then I went to Raleigh, North Carolina, to the beauty school. Your father and mother knew about this and he—your father—helped pay my rent. He didn't help much. Maybe five dollars a week or a month—it was whatever Edith let him have for cigarette money. She always controlled the purse strings."

I nodded at that. "Did she know he was helping you?" I asked.

"No. He said he couldn't let her know. But he came to Raleigh every once in a while to see how I was doing."

Ria talked on about how she finished beauty school, became a very good hair colorist, and had a series of jobs that led to her managing a beauty shop in Chapel Hill, North Carolina. She said she asked my father to stop seeing her during the time she was in beauty school "because I knew my life wouldn't go anywhere with him." She said my father told her that she could never have me, that Edith's name was on the birth certificate. "But he also told me that I would never have to worry about you, because he loved you and you were theirs.

"Edith, your mother, sent me pictures of you at first, up until you were about eight months old. Then she stopped writing. I tried to write her but the letters were always returned. They had moved somewhere. She deliberately did not allow me to get in touch with you from then on. I was still in Chapel Hill, struggling to survive, so I didn't have any way to find out where they went. But I only had fond thoughts of Edith and was very pleased that she was taking such good care of the baby. And I lived the rest of my life thinking that. I had to think that, I guess, in order to survive." Ria's eyes looked deeply into mine, and she extended her hand to touch mine. "But you were always on my mind."

I looked back into her eyes, not knowing what I was feeling. There was so much that she had said.

She squeezed my hand, winked, and smiled at me. "So, that's about it, kid. I went from Chapel Hill to Washington, D.C., to a beauty shop there. Then I went from there to New York City to do the same thing and wound up as a runway and photographic model.

"And that's where I met my first husband, Ross. He was forty years older than me and short, but I thought he was the most fantastic man I had ever met in my life. He was very wealthy, too, although I really didn't know it when I met him. You see,

I was never impressed with wealth. Never, ever. I told him about you before we were married, because I couldn't marry him without letting him know. At the time he seemed to understand, he seemed compassionate. But later . . . oh, well."

"Later what, Ria?"

"Oh, nothing, darling. Just . . . well, sometimes he used it against me. Deep down he was truly Victorian. It turned out that he could never accept that some man had been with me sexually before him. In his final years, when he was out of his mind with uremic poisoning, it became an obsession with him."

"In what way?"

"Oh, I don't think we ever had a fight—even if it was over something as silly as him wanting tuna fish when we were out of it—that he didn't call me a common tramp and throw it in my face that I had had a bastard child.

"But like I told you, I still kept your pictures. I always wondered about you. You can't have a child, no matter what the circumstances, that it doesn't always live with you.

"But I was content. Because there was no way I could have kept you. And there was no way, as long as Ross Hoffman lived, that you would have been allowed in the house."

"Did Janet know about me?"

"Oh, yes. I told her when she was a teen-ager. She had no reaction. All she said was that she knew about it."

When Ria ended her story that Saturday night, we were both exhausted. We both sat silent, neither daring nor caring to look at the other. After a time, she stood up and began to gather her things. I hardly noticed, I was in such a fog. Only when she came and stood by me, running her hand through my hair, did I realize she was leaving. I walked her down the white stucco steps to her Rolls. I started to kiss her good night, and she hugged me to her.

"I'll see you tomorrow?" she said.

"Tomorrow." I smiled.

She pulled away and looked at me almost fearfully. "Are you all right, Jim? Have I done the wrong thing?"

"I'm fine," I said. "You go on home and get some sleep. I'll call you in the morning. I just need to digest what you've told me, you know?"

"I know, dear. I know," she said, kissing me lightly on the lips. "I'll see you tomorrow."

I stood there watching until she had turned south on the Pacific Coast Highway and was out of my sight. Then I slowly made my way back up the steps and into the apartment. I poured a glass of wine and sat back down on the couch. I could hear the surf echoing off the mountain behind me.

The story itself and her performance of it had clearly collided in my mind. I tried to separate the two, to replay the story from beginning to end, stopping it, as one stops a tape recorder, at whatever details seemed important. But there were so many. And there were so few. Intentionally or not, she had edited the story so tightly that even when I was able to go back to a segment and examine it, it was hardly there before it segued into something else. She had shown me the half of my blood that I had never known, the part of me that had been missing all of my life. But I could not touch it. I could not feel it. She had told me of my own father, that portion of my blood that I had known. But again, only glimmers. And the glimmers were mostly ugly and painful.

She had not used the word "rape," but, given her description of what had happened, the term certainly applied. This was the one part of her story that was clear in my mind. I did not think—did not want to think—my father so cold, so brutal as to commit such an act. But here again, she had never quite said he did.

There was a lot that she'd never quite said, leaving me with an overall reaction that was a nonreaction. This seemed like just another in a series of lightning strikes that had been hitting me since Ria had entered my life. And I was numb from them all.

Perhaps, I thought, because of all the magical, rich, and good things that had come into my life along with Ria, I was afraid to react. As I'd realized earlier, I didn't want to question her too closely; I wanted Ria and everything she meant to my life, without any soiled strings of the past attached.

The next morning I called Ria and arranged to meet her around noon at her house. When I got there, she had prepared a pitcher of Bloody Marys and a tray of giant prawns on ice. We took the brunch outside to the patio by the pool. She was bright and prancy, humming a tune and marveling at the beautiful day. I could only shake my head and grin.

She pulled her padded lounge chair into the shade, so as to shield her white skin from the sun, leaned back with her drink, and squinted at me. "Well," she smiled, "how did you like the story?"

"Are you real sure you're not a witch?" I responded.

She laughed. "Why, Jim . . . what do you mean?"

I smiled, shrugging my shoulders. "I don't know. But the more I'm around you, the more unbelievable you become. It's like there's some sort of invincible magic fate that keeps snatching you from the jaws of darkness and placing you, each time, in a jeweled setting."

"Well, darling, it hasn't been all magic, but I say that when there is magic, one really should enjoy it. And that's what I intend to do always. God knows there are enough old fuddy-duddys—and young fuddy-duddys, too—to keep plenty of dark clouds around. I just don't ever intend to be one, or be around one if I can help it."

"I guess I'm a cloud, sometimes," I said. "I sure got in one last night, after you left. It was really eerie."

Her face lost its smile. "I was afraid that might happen. I—"

"No, it wasn't bad," I said. "It was just strange. It was strange hearing so much about me that I don't know. But what really struck me was the path you took—and how I followed that path without ever knowing anything about you. You went from the coast of North Carolina to Raleigh. I did the same. You went from there to New York City and from there to Southern California. I did the same. Considering the circumstances, wouldn't you count that unusual?"

"No," she said, her voice very firm. "Not at all." She tilted her head as though regarding something invisible. "You see, Jim, you were never really meant to be without me. I certainly always knew you were going to show up. It's like I have always known so many things that were destined to happen . . . to me, to those around me. It is a thing that has been with me since I was a little girl." She seemed in a trance now, as she spoke. It was as though some spirit had entered her and was speaking with her lips. Even her voice was different—light, floating, and whispery. Then, as quickly as that persona had come, it left. And she was once again regarding me with a smile and with eyes that were seeing me.

"Anyway, darling," she said, as though nothing had happened, "I've been thinking of something I would very much like to do. I want to give you the birthday party you've never had . . . one that will make up for all of the birthday parties you've never had."

"Sounds good to me," I said, pouring another Bloody Mary.

"Good!" she said, pouring herself one. "Now, let's spend the rest of the day planning it." She hesitated. "And why don't we plan it for next weekend? Will you be free then?"

I nodded. The Bloody Marys and the California sun were working on me, turning me into mush. I looked at the aqua blue pool and pondered how the water would feel. "Okay if I take a swim?" I asked.

"Go right ahead."

"You want to join me?"

She chuckled. "Maybe. But you go on ahead first. I still have my drink to finish."

"Oh, wait a minute," I said. "I didn't bring my suit."

"That doesn't matter," she said. "Nobody's going to see you but me . . . and I'm your mother, darling. I saw you naked before anybody else did."

I went into the house and took my clothes off, wrapping a large towel around me. When I reappeared, Ria was nowhere to be seen. Suddenly her head popped out of the water at the other end of the pool. I looked and her body was a white shimmer under the water line. She seemed to be naked. "Changed my mind," she yelled, grabbing the side of the pool with one hand and using the other to toss back her hair, dark red now, from her face. "Come on in!"

I dropped the towel and walked to the pool's edge. I dove toward her, covering the length of the pool under water. I kept my eyes open and finally spotted her. She had left the side of the pool and was turning a slow somersault underwater. Then she touched bottom with her feet and kicked, sending her body to the surface.

I kicked and came up near her. We swam to the side of the pool and faced each other, my left arm and her right arm draped over the edge. I looked down between us. Her breasts, floating free in the water, were marvels of nature. "Not bad for an old Beverly Hills matron, huh, kid?" she said, grinning, watching me. Then she pushed off the side and dove again, this time toward the other end of the pool. I swam after her and we climbed out of the pool. This time I got a full-length, if brief, look at her body, before she wrapped my towel around herself. Indeed, not bad.

"I'll be right back," she said, and ran into the house. She was gone just a moment and reemerged in a white robe. She tossed me a dry towel, and I wrapped it around me. "Well, I must say one thing," she said. "From the waist down, we're definitely both redheads from the same vat of color."

I laughed, blushing at the same time.

"I just can't figure out what happened to the hair on your head," she said teasingly. "Mine stayed red and yours, except for your beard, turned brown."

I looked at her in mock seriousness. "Yeah, I've been thinking about doing an investigative piece on that. Probably something to do with—"

"Clean living dear." She laughed. "And maybe just the smallest little smidgen of modern chemistry."

It was late afternoon before we finally went inside and changed back into our clothes again. As we were having a cocktail at the bar, Ria asked me what I wanted most for the special birthday party. I told her I hadn't the foggiest idea. "I know," she finally said. "How about a weekend in San Francisco?"

"I would love that."

"Good. That's what we'll do. It's one of my absolutely favorite cities, and there's this adorable little hotel I know that's right in the middle of things. I'll make our reservations tomorrow. You're going to have to have your tux and your dark blue suit ready and . . ." On a bar napkin she jotted down a list of apparel necessities and tucked it into my shirt pocket. "Kid," she grinned, "we're going to have ourselves a ball!"

The flight from Los Angeles to San Francisco takes about an hour. I had made the trip many times, but only in the line of duty. For me, San Francisco had always been merely a jumping-off point for a story. The last jump I'd made had been to infiltrate San Quentin's prison guards and find out what it was like to be caught in the middle of a black militants' prison revolt. I was remembering that on the last Friday in June, as Ria and I boarded a PSA jet for San Francisco. I settled back in my seat, and suddenly I felt her hand gripping mine tightly. I looked over at her, and her eyes were shut. The color had left her face.

"Are you all right?" I asked.

Biting her lips and keeping her eyes closed, she nodded. The plane began to move, heading for the runway. Her hand was gripping mine even harder now. When the engine began that caterwauling sound that signaled takeoff, her nails were digging little red lines in the flesh of my palm. The plane leapt forward. She was squeezing my hand so hard my fingers were going numb. Only when the plane began to level did Ria's grip loosen and her eyes begin to open. A stewardess was passing by, and Ria grabbed her by the hand. "Double vodka on the rocks," she said. "Quick."

I leaned over and looked at her. "Hi!" I said cheerfully. "You there?"

She cut her eyes ever so slightly to meet mine. "I'd forgotten," she finally said, "how much I absolutely hate flying. It's just a nightmare . . . totally, totally a nightmare!" By the time the drink wagon wheeled by, Ria was ready for another double. I had one too, sipping mine slowly while she gulped hers down.

When the seat belt and no smoking signs blinked on, Ria's body went rigid again and her right hand began its death grip on my left. Once we were in the terminal, however, she quickly transformed herself into Miss Dynamite again, sweeping through the San Francisco terminal as if she owned it, riding the moving belt transporter as if it were a red carpet laid down in her honor.

The longest, blackest Mercedes limousine I'd ever seen was waiting outside and Ria steered me to it. A tall, middle-aged black man dressed in chauffeur's uniform opened the rear door and beckoned us to step in. Ria handed him our tickets, and he soon returned with our luggage and loaded it into the trunk. "Well, now," Ria said as we pulled away from the terminal and began speeding toward the city, "this is more like it. Now," she said, looking at me, "are you ready to have the most absolutely gorgeous time of your life?" I ran my fingertips along the leather interior of the car, and looked out through the smoked window glass. I was having a wonderful time already.

As we drove up one of the steeper hills of the city, I saw the Mark Hopkins Hotel and asked if we were going to be staying there. To me, the Mark Hopkins epitomized what was classy in San Francisco.

"Darling, no!" Ria exclaimed. "Not that dreary monster."

The limo finally pulled up to a handsome two-story building that looked more like a private home than a hotel. The bespectacled gentleman at the desk gushed over our arrival. "Oh, yes, Mrs. Dammeron. We have been waiting for you. Everything," he said, "is as you requested." We boarded a small elevator, which quietly ascended to the second floor. The porter led us to the end of a hall, where he opened a door. We walked into a world of Victorian elegance. The carpet seemed bottomless as I stepped inside. We appeared to be in an elaborately furnished living room. "There aren't any beds," I said to Ria.

She winked at the porter, who seemed to find something funny in my observation, and tipped him as he handed her three keys. When he left, closing the door behind him, she handed me two of them. "This one is for the door we just came in, and this one is for your bedroom," she said.

"Where's that?" I asked.

"Over there," she said, pointing to one end of the room. "It has a king-size bed. My bedroom is over there," she said, gesturing with her head at the other end of the large room. She looked at me in an odd sort of way. "Jim, darling, have you never been in a suite before?"

"Oh! Right!" I said, the obvious suddenly dawning on me. "Of course! A suite." I looked at her somewhat sheepishly. "I was wondering where the porter disappeared to with our luggage."

"Jim, you're teasing me." She laughed.

I shrugged, smiling. "Ria, you gotta remember something about me. Up until now, Holiday Inns have been 'top of the line' for me."

She walked over and put her arms around me, hugging me to her. "Well, kid. Not anymore." She stepped back, placing her hands on her hips and tilting her head to one side in her familiar fashion. "Now, why don't you go have a shower and get dressed. I'll do the same. We've got an hour before our dinner reservation at the Blue Fox."

That night and the subsequent day could have passed for an introductory course in hedonism. Ria quickly shed any semblance of her Beverly Hills society self and behaved like a woman bent on having a terrific time. What had been billed as my party very quickly became "our" party.

I complained not, for it was an insanely lovely experience. Everywhere we went, people stared at Ria's beauty, and I enjoyed their envy. Ria's purse was a bottomless well, and whatever I saw and wanted, I got, whether it was an extra double order of a special abalone dish or a gold ring that caught my fancy. She was in charge. All I did was tag along happily like a three-year-old, telling her whenever I spied something I liked. It went on like that, nonstop.

On Sunday afternoon we finally slept. I barely remember showering before I was in my bed sound asleep. When I awoke, it was already sundown. I lay in bed lazily, laughing to myself as I somewhat groggily recalled the pace we had been maintaining.

My bedroom door opened slightly.

"Jim, are you awake?"

"Arggg," I replied in mock anguish. "No more! No more! I surrender, ma'am."

She laughed and came into the room. "Move over," she commanded, and sat down beside me on the bed. She was wearing a sheer night gown and I could see the outline of her body beneath the fabric. I was naked under the covers. I sensed the strangest, most delicious feeling of tension between us. I rolled onto my side and reached across her for my cigarettes, which were on the side table. My arm rubbed against her. She didn't pull back. Instead she took my beard between her thumb and forefinger and gave it a yank.

A knock sounded at the living room door. "That must be my surprise for you," she said, slipping out of the room. I lay back, smoking my cigarette, and listened to her talking with someone. Then I heard a cork pop and a bottle being cradled in ice. The living room door closed.

She reappeared, pushing my door open with a silver tray. "We're going to play at home tonight," she said. She set the tray beside me in the middle of the bed. There was a mountain of caviar, accompanied by chopped egg and onion and small pieces of toast. She left again, returning with a jeroboam of champagne and two long-stemmed glasses. "We turn back into pumpkins tomorrow, kid," she said, pouring our glasses full. "I thought a private party might be in order tonight. Happy birthday," she whispered, kissing me and then popping a toast piled with caviar into my mouth.

"How do you feel, Jim?" she asked, turning her lovely face to me.

"Great," I said. "Absolutely, wickedly, wonderfully great."

She lay on her side, propping herself up on her elbow. "I mean," she said mischievously, touching her finger to the tip of my nose, "how do you feel about me?" She moved her finger from my nose and placed it on my chest. "Well?" she asked.

I started laughing softly and shaking my head. "You know," I said, "that this is stark, raving crazy, don't you?"

"Uh-huh," she said softly, her eyes still blazing away at me. "Now tell me, how do you feel about me?"

"I . . . uh . . . feel," I said, moving my left hand to touch a lock of her hair that had fallen across the middle of her forehead, "like we ought to have another bottle of champagne."

Her finger traced a line across my chest as she rolled away from me quickly, sliding from the bed to the floor. I scrambled after her. She giggled and got up and ran into the living room. I was right behind her when I suddenly realized I didn't have any clothes on. I stopped short at the door of the bedroom and poked my head out. "What are you doing?" I asked.

"Get back in bed," she said, "I'll be right back."

I stayed at the door, watching her disappear into the kitchen. Then I heard a cork pop, and she rounded the corner with another jeroboam of champagne. There was perhaps thirty feet between us, and when she saw me still there looking at her, she halted, lifted the bottle to her lips, and took a long drink. Then she lowered the bottle from her mouth and placed it on the floor. She began moving in slow pirouettes. Then, raising her arms, she stopped mid-swirl and sank down onto the carpet. She reached for the bottle again and took a long drink. This time the champagne spilled from her lips and ran down the front of her gown, wetting it. She glanced down, then back at me. "I thought I told you to stay in bed," she whispered.

"I wouldn't have missed what I just saw for the world," I said. "You're—"

"Sshh," she said, putting a finger to her lips. "Now get back in bed." I turned and did as I was told. I lay waiting for her. Moments passed, and my mind was whirling. What in the hell was happening? Things were getting crazier and crazier. Everything seemed totally out of control.

She came in the room, holding the bottle. She sat on the bed and filled our glasses with champagne. "Now," she said, "as I was saying, how do you feel about me?"

Both wired and tired, I thought, as though a long journey in the dark had finally, happily been ended. "I've been needing you," I told her. "I've been needing you for a long, long time."

101

She put her arms around my neck. "Well, Jim, now you've got me."

# Chapter 7

The summer of 1973 blurred swiftly into fall. Ria and I were inseparable. We both knew that what we were doing was probably not best for either of us, but for several months we did not deal with this bothersome feeling. I, for one, felt good about our relationship. It gave me a sense of well-being. That outweighed everything else.

It was Ria who, just before Thanksgiving, admitted that perhaps we were becoming too close for her comfort.

"I'm beginning to feel a case of guilties, Jim," she told me one Saturday over lunch at a private beach club in Malibu.

"I'm sorry, Ria. What did you say?" I asked. I had been watching two young women seated at the table behind her, straining to catch the intriguing conversation they seemed to be having.

"I said if you'd get your mind off those two girls behind me, you would hear what I was saying," she said somewhat petulantly.

"I'm sorry," I repeated. "Getting half-smashed by midday is

still new to me, and sometimes I just drift out to sea." I smiled. "Forgive me?"

She spoke again, in an uncharacteristically low voice. "I said I'm beginning to feel a case of the guilties."

"Over what?"

"Over us. I'm not so sure we should be spending so much time together. Now don't misunderstand me, Jim. I enjoy being around you very much. Perhaps . . . too much. But, darling, I should be dating older men and you should be dating younger women. People are going to start noticing that you and I are spending an inordinate amount of time together, and they're going to start drawing some conclusions that would be absolutely devastating to me. I think some already are thinking those things. And I know—and you know—that Janet is not liking it one bit."

I listened to her words and heard her concern. But I didn't feel it myself. Our closeness since the San Francisco birthday party had been like a warm, soothing panacea that was making up for all the years I had spent without her and in need of her . . . indeed, starved for her. She had been thwarted in her natural maternal desire, her physical need, to mother her baby; I had been that baby, deprived of that essential physical contact. I didn't need a psychoanalyst to tell me that the bonding urge between mother and child could be very strong even after more than three decades.

But part of it, I had to admit, was the pure male-female attraction that we had both felt for each other from the beginning. We had both fought it, both tried to submerge it in our other feelings for each other. I had never tried to put it out of my mind that Ria was my mother—far from it. Discovering my real mother after all these years was just too important to me; I wouldn't put it aside for a moment. Sexual attraction was one of my feelings about her, but not the most important. Because I thought I had it all in perspective, my sexual feelings for Ria never bothered me. They seemed a natural part of our complicated response to each other.

But there was something that *did* bother me. Every so often

I got a glimmering that Ria was responding not so much to me, but to whatever traces of my father were in me. I didn't like facing that possibility. It gave me a weird feeling of jealousy, but even more than that, it raised questions about Ria's story of my birth.

That day at my apartment she had denied ever loving my father, ever having what might be called a real relationship with him. Their sexual relations had been rather brutal and almost impersonal. Yet sometimes when she and I were together she spoke of him fondly, almost wistfully. One night she told me that he had written her a poem, and she had kept it over all these years. She had asked me if I wanted to read it. I found this rather remarkable and somewhat disturbing—her cherishing a poem written by a man she had virtually called a rapist. I politely deferred reading it. In reality, I did not want to see it ever.

"Well, Jim?" Ria's voice penetrated my thoughts.

"Well, I don't . . . I don't think you should be feeling the guilties, as you put it. I mean, we haven't done anything that I would consider wrong, Ria. We've just been making up for a lot of lost time. And you can't say that you haven't been enjoying it, can you?"

"No," she said, "I can't say I haven't enjoyed being with you, nor can I say that there has been anything really wrong. Not wrong to us. But, Jim, we should be thinking about what other people might say."

"I don't give a damn what other people might say. Hell, it's natural for us to be spending a lot of time together, just because of our circumstances."

She stiffened at my words. "You don't understand, Jim. I have to be concerned with what other people say. I live in a goldfish bowl. I am a prominent socialite. I enjoy that. It's as important to me as writing is to you. And, darling, there are those in my world who would take delight in destroying that. I just can't take that risk."

"So what do we do?" I asked.

"I don't know," she said. Then she smiled again. "It's just

something I needed to talk to you about. We'll see how things go."

As we left the table after lunch, I glanced back at the two girls who were still deeply engaged in conversation. "I really feel sorry for those two," I said to Ria.

"Why?"

"Well, I was listening to them when you were visiting your friends at that other table, and it seems both of those girls are married and apparently quite well off, yet neither of them can find a good couple to be friends with."

Ria regarded me curiously. "What did they say, exactly?"

"Well, you know—how 'terribly hard' it was these days to find a good couple. Seems they no sooner find one than they lose them."

"Darling, you're not serious, are you?" She was laughing.

"I'm just telling you what they said. They were really upset about it. One of them said it was driving her to tears."

Ria was laughing so hard her body was shaking. "Dear," she said, "they were talking about servants."

Thanksgiving that year was to be a "family" get-together at at Ria's winter home in Palm Springs. Janet spent every holiday with her mother, often in Palm Springs, but this year she declined Ria's invitation, saying she had already committed herself to another engagement. The news set Ria off and I, having failed in my efforts to lure Janet into so much as a lunch, much less a friendship, did little to speak in her defense. More and more I was coming to resent my half sister's standoffishness. I mentioned this to Ella, Ria's housekeeper, one afternoon when Ria was attending an auction to benefit one of the seven charitable groups to which she belonged. Ella, whose voice was almost honey coated, shook her head when I remarked that Janet was being something of a twit.

"Jim, now I don't want to say there's nothing wrong with Janet's way of acting right now, cause it would be real nice if she would be friendlier toward you. But the thing is, she's been Mrs. Dammeron's only child for a long time. And, now don't you tell

106

Mrs. Dammeron I told you this, but you see, the two of them hasn't always been real close—like you'd think a mother and daughter would.

"I know I remember when Janet was a little girl and Mrs. Dammeron, she was taking care of her first husband, Janet's father, who was dying. And, well, things was kind of bad around here then. Janet's father never did give her much time, even when he was well. Oh, he'd buy her anything she wanted, but he was always too busy to see much of her. Anyways, it seem like Janet started resenting her mother spending all that time with her father. And then, Mrs. Dammeron, she couldn't do much about it because Mr. Hoffman, he was a very demanding man of her.

"And then you come along." Ella laughed softly. "Well, now then Mrs. Dammeron turns every bit of her attention on you, cause you is her long-lost baby. And, well, you know, that don't help matters out too much with Janet."

Listening to Ella, I knew she was trying her best to make me understand a situation and be more compassionate. But I found it difficult. The matter seemed more complicated than Ella thought. Janet had grown up, according to Ria, overhearing her father curse me for a bastard child who would never be permitted to set foot in his home, and I sensed that she herself had adopted his attitude. She saw herself as the princess, the heir apparent, and I—in the vernacular of my native land—was trash, and poor trash at that. I couldn't say that for sure, because Janet had yet to say a harsh word to me. But that imperious attitude was there. There was an anger birthing inside of me; I was being looked down upon and condemned because of a circumstance not of my own making.

As it turned out, I would have done better to bow out of the Thanksgiving celebration myself. The weekend was my first real look at Palm Springs, and, at least from my vantage point, it was nothing but Beverly Hills with sand. Certainly the restaurants and the stores were replicas of those on Rodeo Drive. The only difference was that in the desert, the plutocrats tended to go out less, preferring to isolate themselves in elaborately protected compounds. Ria's compound was a haven for corporate heads and old Beverly Hills money, a combination that did not overlap with the television and movie set, or with the doctor-lawyer set, or with recording industry executives and their stars. Wherever we went I was the youngest person there, by at least ten years.

Thanksgiving in Palm Springs also turned out to be my first encounter with ironclad rules of behavior and dress. When Ria began to describe them to me, I laughed, thinking she was having fun with me. She quickly and firmly assured me this was no laughing matter. "This is a very exclusive club, Jim," she said. "The waiting list is endless. The rules here were established long ago to insure that a certain amount of propriety is always observed." I wasn't sure about the propriety. But at last I learned where it was that I would be wearing the white shoes Veronica had selected for me . . . and the white slacks . . . and the rather horrible checkered coat.

Back in Los Angeles, Ria had announced that I was to be her escort for the parties she would be giving and attending through Christmas and New Year's. "Now, Jim," she said, in the tone I had come to associate with an impending lecture, "I want you to look your absolute best, so you must trim your beard and moustache and, for God's sake, darling, get rid of those horrible wire-rimmed glasses you wear. They make you look twenty years older." She regarded me wickedly. "After all, one must not hide one's good looks. I certainly will not be hiding mine."

I did as she bade. I needed my glasses at work, but it was easy enough to do without them in the evening. Trimming my hair and beard didn't bother me much. No matter how short they were, I would still be the only bearded person at whatever party we attended.

Finally she deemed me fit, proper, and ready. And we began the endless parties. I learned very quickly that Ria was my social antitype. If there was such a thing as a social blossom, she was an extravagant bouquet. I saw immediately why she was so popular and in demand. In a world consisting mostly of corporate wives with frosted hair and frozen mannerisms, she was a hot flame that never flickered. What I couldn't understand was why she wasted her vivacity on such a boring crowd.

At first I hesitated to tell Ria how unexciting I found her circle to be. But eventually I was driven to. "Come on, Ria, fess up," I said. "Don't you find some of these things boring, too?"

"Darling, of course they are. You will continue to meet some of the most boring people in the world—absolute experts at it! But they aren't the party. You are. And I am. Wherever we go."

And so we went. Despite her "case of the guilties," Ria occupied every moment of my free time for the entire month of December. Officially I was still her brother, a deception that went unrevealed. People not only bought the story, but applauded it. Some actually asked if we were twins. We were a big success, and I even discovered a way of enjoying myself. The secret, it turned out, was never to be too sober or too drunk.

Once I had achieved this perfect state, I found myself capable of socializing in ways I never had before. I danced with Ria and other women until the wee hours of the morning, when, in fact, I had not been on a dance floor in twelve years. I learned the art of chitchat, which was to me a foreign language. The secret was simple, Ria said. "Just say a little to everyone you're introduced to, but say it beautifully and without it meaning a damn thing."

I did as I was told and it seemed to work. Being introduced as a writer for the *Times* made it even easier. For some reason these people seemed thrilled to associate a face with the name they had been seeing in the paper. I wasn't sure why people of such wealth and social standing should feel that way, but I certainly didn't object to a little adulation. When my name started to appear in the society column for the *Times,* I did begin to get a little edgy at work, but my fears of being ridiculed by the city room bunch were groundless. Nobody there ever read the society column.

My favorite party of the season was held at a monstrously big mansion that one of Ria's friends called home. The house, we were told, had cost 10 million dollars, and during the cocktail hour the host gave some of us a guided tour. The first three floors were the usual collection of elaborately furnished bedrooms, bathrooms, and walk-in closets the size of my former house in the Valley. Then we were led belowstairs, to admire a subterranean swimming pool, a cellar stocked with one thousand cases of fine wines, and a marble-floored ballroom large enough to accommodate three hundred people.

Janet and Ronald crossed paths with us at a few of these affairs. Ronald wisely kept his distance, although it was clear he wasn't afraid to face me. More disturbing was that Janet seemed removed from me as well. We would be at the same party, dancing on the same floor, but if I happened to look her way, she would turn her head or simply look through me. One night I learned the reason why.

We were at a party in Beverly Hills and Ria introduced me to a group of young people whom she identified as Janet's friends. Later on I was taken aside by one young lady who seemed unusually interested in me. As the conversation continued, I broke one of the rules and drank more than was good for a party tongue.

"You know, of course," the girl said, as though she and I were confidants, "that you are a very big threat to Janet."

"No, I didn't," I replied, but I remembered Ella explaining how jealous Janet was of her mother's affection.

"Oh, yes," the girl said. "Janet is running scared that you'll intrude on her inheritance."

"Janet? You're kidding." The girl assured me she was not. "Look," I said, the liquor now in full control, "I'm Janet's uncle for Christ's sake. How th' hell would I be that kind of threat to her?"

"Janet says you're her half brother." The girl smiled. "But don't worry, we'll keep it in the family."

Encouraged by her friendliness, I picked up another drink and motioned her toward a door that led outside to a rose garden. We found a stone wall to lean on and stood there, looking out across the manicured lawn to Los Angeles, miles below.

"Look," I said to her, "I'm gonna tell you something that's just between you and me. Okay?"

She nodded.

"I've been in Ria's will since the day she made one. And there's nothing Janet or anybody else can do about that. But

110

that's just Ria's personal will. The Hoffman trust, which Janet and Ria live on, is another matter. I'm not part of that. Janet doesn't have a damn thing to worry about."

We returned to the party. I was getting madder by the minute. I had never believed that Janet really felt this way, and I sure as hell didn't expect to hear about it from a total stranger. I found it hard to believe that Janet was letting money—which she already had plenty of—stand between us, and I wanted to go to her right then and find out what was happening. But Ria saw me and whirled me onto the dance floor. Across the floor Janet was dancing too.

I didn't mention the matter to Ria. But then, I really didn't have to. That something had suddenly, seriously gone wrong between Janet and me soon became apparent. My good "friend" at the party apparently went straight to Janet with news of our conversation. I don't know what her version of it was; perhaps she claimed I had been boasting of being in Ria's will. Whatever the case, from then on Janet was furious at me and openly hostile to Ria.

The Beverly Hills grapevine was cruel. And I had been naïve. It was foolish of me to confide in a stranger, yet it hadn't occurred to me that anyone would deliberately seek me out in order to set me up. Nor had it occurred to me that Janet would tell her mother's secret to an acquaintance, or that she and her whole set would see me as a fortune-hunting interloper. Indeed, there was a lot that had never occurred to me.

It was at this point that Janet embarked on a new campaign. Whereas before we had hardly ever seen her, now she camped more and more at Ria's home, harping at her about me. Distraught, Ria would relay Janet's accusations to me. I would deny them, console her, and then the whole thing would start all over again.

Some of her tricks were petty but annoying nonetheless. Invariably now, on evenings or afternoons when I came to visit Ria or pick her up, Janet's Jaguar, like an extension of her anger, would be blocking the way to the inner courtyard. Inside the house she would not acknowledge my presence. If I walked in while she and Ria were talking, Ria would look up and say, "Well, Jim, hi. Janet and I are just having a little chat." But Janet would not look at me. Instead, she would stop talking and look the other way in silence.

At first I let her have her way. But increasingly I came to resent her childish attempts at intimidation. I would walk in, and as she turned away I would say, "Janet, could I have the keys to your car? You're blocking my way." Without a word she would storm out, get in her car, and roar away.

Ria tried to act as if she didn't take Janet's behavior all that seriously. But more and more I saw the hurt it was causing her. And more and more, I tried to gear my arrivals to Janet's absences. It was useless. The girl seemed to have radar.

Finally I lost my temper. One evening I called her. "Janet, I don't know what your problem is, but you seem determined to upset Ria and wreck everything around her. Now you're not intimidating me one goddamn bit, but Ria is very fragile right now because of Dave. And I would think you, as her daughter, would have regard for her feelings. But no, you keep acting like a spoiled two-year-old. What th' fuck's wrong with you?"

There was a silence at her end.

"Janet?"

"What," she finally replied in a cold, measured tone, "would you know?" And she hung up the phone.

That night I lay in bed listening to Janet's voice repeat her question. The more I listened, the angrier I became. What would I know?

I knew one thing. I knew then I would never make peace with Janet because for some reason, as I'd sensed earlier, she really did see me not only as a threat to her money, but as some piece of common trash as well. She held herself so high above me. What I had tried to tell myself was country boy paranoia had turned out to be the truth.

I slept badly that night. One dream kept coming back over and over again. In it I saw Janet, stripped of her Adolfo sports clothes and her Italian shoes, dressed in jeans, sweatshirt, and worn tennis shoes . . . hungry, penniless, and without one friend in the world. I saw her over and over again, each time in a different place—standing on a corner of Bragg Boulevard in Fayetteville, North Carolina, while dozens of 82nd Airborne paratroopers surrounded her, leering, farting, and pinching her breasts . . . or walking down main street in Butte, Montana, catching the hard-eyed looks of the copper cowboys . . . or standing outside an employment office—anywhere.

And in each scene, she would see me and come running, begging me to help her, to protect her. And I would just look at her, shrug my shoulders, and say, "But Janet, what would I know?"

After New Year's, Ria and I went to fewer and fewer parties, which was perfectly fine with me. But as the first months of 1974 went by, I found Ria less and less enthusiastic about the time we spent together. Without ever discussing it, we had put aside the sexual feelings we had had for each other. But that was not what was bothering me. Ria just seemed to be losing her spirit.

I blamed Janet for it and mentioned that to Ria one evening.

"No, Jim, that's not totally true," she said as we retired to the library for afterdinner drinks. "Janet isn't helping matters, but the truth is, darling, I'm lonely . . . very lonely. This is a big house to be alone in . . . particularly when you're fifty-two years old and widowed twice in the space of five years."

"But Ria, you look thirty-nine. You're still one helluva good-looking woman. You're going to have men beating down your door."

She regarded me with a wry smile. "Jim, let me tell you something about the society I live in. There aren't many available men. Most of those who aren't married are either gay or fortune hunters. I should know. I found out the hard way after my first husband died. And so, you are left with your friends. Except suddenly you find that the friends you had when you were mar-ried, well, darling, they just sort of disappear. The women forget to include you on their invitation lists. The prettier you are, the faster you're forgotten. Their husbands just might find you more attractive than they are. And they live in absolute fear of that.

113

At least, most of them do. And you find yourself spending more and more lonely hours at home."

She grimaced. "The only reason I was invited to all the holiday parties was because of you. Having you as my escort rendered me safe.

"Oh, Jim," she said, suddenly crying. "I am so afraid of being alone. I've been alone all of my life. My first husband was forty years older than me and I spent the last twelve years of his life alone, watching him die. I was too young to have been forced to do that. I sat in this house and watched the world pass me by. And now this. The same thing again. Only I'm not that young anymore. I'm just old enough to be a threat to nearly every woman I know in Beverly Hills."

"Ria," I said, "why lock yourself into Beverly Hills? Why don't you expand your horizons a little? You're only a couple of miles from UCLA. Why not take some courses there? You'd have a ball. And you'd be around different, interesting people of all ages. Or, hell, you could even take a nice cruise somewhere. Shipboard romances can be pretty neat. I used to meet all kinds of fascinating single people in Fort Lauderdale when the Pacific & Orient cruise ships would dock there for the weekend."

She looked up at me, brushing her tears away. "You're right, kid," she said, managing a smile, "why should I stay locked up here?"

"Well," I said, holding her hands, "remember this too. You've got me. And between us, we ought to be able to find someone pretty spectacular for you."

But we didn't. Slowly, I learned that Ria would not even try to escape the boundaries of Beverly Hills. I spent many evenings and weekends with her, but nothing I said or suggested could budge her from a routine that was almost guaranteed to keep her lonely. I invited her to go to the movies with me. Her response: "They don't make good movies anymore. All you see now is trash." I invited her to concerts at the Hollywood Bowl. Her response: "You go ahead, darling. . . . I can't stand sitting on those hard seats." She refused to go anywhere but to her established list of bistros where she would be seated at the same table,

114

fawned over by the same maitre d', and served the same food. She seldom ate it now, however, preferring more and more simply to sit there, sip vodka, and talk to me. The talk was always the same talk, too. It was as if her whole life had consisted of giving birth to me and rediscovering me.

I began to tire of the routine, and Ria began to tire of my attempts to budge her from her tiny world. After several months of this stalemate, she decided that it was time for me to begin dating some of the daughters of her society friends. While she never said this in so many words, she seemed to feel that she had groomed me as well as anyone could, trained me in the ways of polite society, and now I should address myself seriously to marrying into some of the local money. What she did say was that people who saw us together so often—whether they knew I was her son or thought I was her brother—might get "the wrong impression." This was the same worry she had confided to me months ago, at the beach club. I hadn't taken it too seriously then, and Ria hadn't seemed to, either, what with her constantly inviting me to holiday parties where everyone would see us together. Now I understood her reason for inviting me—so she could gain entrée to the social season.

To please Ria, I did not resist her matchmaking scheme. I didn't think it would work, but if it did, hell, I'd be rich. The first candidate was from "old money," I was told. Her father was a famous engineer, her mother a noted sculptor. They lived in San Marino, a moneyed bastion next to Pasadena. The girl was an artist and illustrator who free-lanced for magazines. Ria arranged for us to meet at her home one evening. There would be cocktails and dinner and the rest of the evening would be left up to us.

I arrived a little late. Ria and her other guest were comfortably arranged at the bar and apparently enjoying each other's company. I joined them. The girl was striking, the blind date of one's dreams. Tall and very well-proportioned, she had red-blond hair, pale skin, and green eyes. Through her well-bred, ladylike demeanor I detected an earthiness that was very attractive. The three of us chitted and chatted through dinner and I managed

115

to tell a few tales of the *Times* that seemed to hold the young lady's attention. Finally, Ria stifled a yawn. "I'm going to let you kids go on," she said, apparently convinced that she had, indeed, made a good match. She hugged us both and retired.

The girl looked at me demurely. "Well, what shall we do now?" she asked.

"It's early," I said. "Would you like to follow me out to Malibu and have a few drinks at my place?"

She thought for a moment, then replied, "Sounds delightful. Haven't been to Malibu in eons."

We walked outside to where her car was parked on the graceful, curved drive. As I opened the door for her, she tossed her handbag into the front seat and threw her arms around me.

"Grrrrr," she said, baring her magnificently orthodontured Beverly Hills teeth ferociously. Then she kissed me, just as ferociously. The forward motion of her attack threw me off balance and the two of us fell over the azalea hedge bordering Ria's drive, landing on the strip of grass that ran between the drive and the street. She wound up on top and continued her assault, her dress riding up over her thighs as she straddled my legs and began undoing my belt and zipper.

Now, this was really decadence, I thought cheerfully—losing my trousers in the bright light of a sodium streetlamp, at the curb of one of the most traveled streets in Beverly Hills, only thirty feet from my own mother's front door. My partner's growls became louder and more frequent until we climaxed, and she stopped growling long enough to sink her teeth right through my shirt and into the flesh of my shoulder. For a moment we just lay on the lawn panting, then suddenly we both began laughing, frantically covering each other's mouths with our hands.

When the laughter subsided, we began straightening our clothes. "James, darling," she said in an affected tone not unlike Ria's British accent voice, "I am sooo delighted that you came. We must do this again sometime. It's been absolutely marvy."

"Yes," I replied. "Quite. Actually."

I grinned all the way back to Malibu, but as it turned out, our affair was short-lived. She got a job with a Paris fashion maga-

116

zine several weeks later. Again, Ria riffled through her personal blue book. I, meanwhile, rested.

Ria's next choice was a different type, but equally attractive— a rangy, freckled redhead whose parents had been neighbors of Ria's for years before moving to Santa Barbara. Recently divorced from a well-known sports announcer, she impressed me immediately with her warmth, her sense of humor, and her determination to be independent of her family's rather stifling wealth. Or so she said.

We began dating, but I soon realized I could not afford her. Although she worked as an assistant to a landscape architect, she still drew a monthly trust fund stipend of five thousand dollars, and she lived in a style that devoured every penny of it. Since five thousand dollars was about one-fourth of my annual salary at the *Times,* I quickly became hard-pressed to keep things going. The girl assumed, of course, that I was as wealthy as Ria was. When I broke the news of my meager salary and asked if we could tailor our activities to my bank book, she basically disappeared.

Undiscouraged, Ria produced several other candidates; none of them, of course, worked out. One girl had a love affair with cocaine that was staggering both in financial and physical terms. She liked the "high" of dealing it, as well as snorting it, and what time I spent with her I lived in constant fear. A hard-drug bust I didn't need. Another girl checked out fine on all points until we got to my bedroom in Malibu where she undressed, reached in her purse, and plugged a vibrator into a wall socket. I could have her, she said, as soon as she got off on the vibrator. She couldn't get off without it, she said.

"But they're from the best of families," Ria said, when I told her to throw away the blue book.

"Ria," I said, "with very rare exceptions they are all screwed-up, spoiled little pains in the ass. I appreciate your efforts, but I think I'll go it on my own for a while."

I retreated to Malibu, bought a bicycle, and pursued the social possibilities that abounded within a mile, north or south, of my apartment.

I continued to see Ria. I would escort her to dinner a couple of times a week and then return to her home for a nightcap. But our relationship was seriously deteriorating now, and there were obvious dissatisfactions on both sides. On my side, I was upset because it seemed to me there were at least two Rias I was dealing with. One was the down-to-earth, practical, yet compassionate and giving Ria. She was mostly visible in the mornings and afternoons as she set about overseeing the physical maintenance of her estate, handling trust fund business at her worktable, and doing a variety of chores that required a clear, sharp mind and common sense. I felt comfortable with this Ria. If I dropped by in the mornings—usually just for a cup of coffee before heading downtown for work—we would talk about everything from a funny human interest story in the *Times* to the intricacies of the stock market. We would talk about going back, together, to the town where Ria had been born so I could meet the other side of my family. We would talk about my work, and she would tell me how much she believed in my talent and in my future.

These morning talks were something I looked forward to. I felt at ease with her then. I felt more like her son. But they became fewer and fewer, and Ria mostly found time for me only in the evening, when it was time to go out. She would have a drink or two and then emerge as the wildly flamboyant Society Ria who literally charged into the night. Already bored with this, I came to dislike it . . . and her. She suddenly seemed too loud, too happy, too rich, and too given to doing the little things that I was learning the overprivileged usually get away with. This was the Ria who, if she didn't think she was given the right table at a restaurant, would gripe about it the rest of the night. This was the Ria who would look at a fancy menu and then order a hamburger, complaining loudly that the food was lousy anyway. This was the Ria who, with each additional drink, would become more and more catty, pointing to other people in a restaurant and talking about their lack of "real money" and the fact that "she" had had a dozen face-lifts or "he" was a bastard who had really put the rush on her once, but fortunately she had found out in time that he was really just trying to get her money. This

118

was also the Ria who, in front of a hundred people, would start talking noisily about how psychic she was. Or who would start singing at the top of her voice, waving her arms in the air and shaking her body.

At times her actions bothered me so much that I would try, as tactfully as I could, to get her down from the horse she was riding and back to earth with me. Mainly I did this when she seemed to be about two seconds away from jumping on top of the table and breaking into a can-can.

"Ria," I would whisper, "can we go now?"

And her reply would be a little snort. "Oh, Grandpa," she would say derisively. "Time to get old Grandpa to bed." After we got home, she would accuse me of spoiling her evening, of not letting her have any fun.

She started doing something else then, both in public and in private. She began to criticize me openly. At first it was in the form of subtle little digs. Then things became not so subtle: I was gaining too much weight. . . . I wasn't keeping my beard trimmed as neatly as I should have.

At first, I let these things pass. Because, in fact, what she was saying was true. I had gained considerable weight since meeting her, even though it was mostly due to the self-indulgent style of living she had been affording me. And my beard, as well as my hair, was longer. I was letting both grow . . . for no reason that I knew of. But then the scope of her criticism broadened, and she began to launch into me about other things.

"Jim," she said one evening, "why do you treat Janet the way you do? She is basically a good, sweet person. Yet you won't give her a chance. You used to be very nice to her, but now you won't speak to her, you won't look at her when she's here, and you're always making very critical remarks about her to other people.

"And why have you treated all of those lovely little girls the way you have? They say you just dumped them without a word. Several of them were almost in tears when they told me how you treated them. You know, my dear, you're rapidly getting the reputation of being quite a bastard."

I swirled the drink in my glass, trying to come up with an

119

explanation that would make sense to Ria. But too many drinks that night had loosened the ties on my old temper.

"Frankly, Ria, the girls you've introduced me to have been a bunch of elegant freaks. I tried relating to them, but the only common ground was sex. And even in bed they were freakier than I was comfortable with.

"Then there's the matter of money. They have it and I don't. But they expect me to have it. And they don't relate to full-time jobs. They expect me to be able to just take off and go somewhere anytime they feel like it. And I, in turn, cannot relate all that well to somebody who goes through life perfectly satisfied to suck on their trust fund's sugar tit."

"Well, Jim," Ria said, staring somewhat coldly at me, "if you hadn't blown the money I gave you on that silly Porsche and instead invested it in the stocks my financial consultant suggested to you, you might have some money right now, wouldn't you?"

"I don't think you understand how much owning that Porsche means to me," I replied. "In fact, I'm beginning to wonder if you understand me much at all."

"Well, you may be right," she said. "I certainly don't understand this war you are waging with Janet."

"You don't? Well, let me tell you something, Ria. She started the damn war."

"I know she did, Jim. But you have to understand that it isn't easy for her to accept you just like that."

"She did at first."

"She tried, poor girl. She tried very hard. But you just walked in here and, as far as she is concerned, tried to take over everything. I'm caught in the middle of it, frankly. And you could help matters a great deal if you would be nicer to her."

"Ria, Janet is a spoiled, conniving little bitch. She hates me, and she hates you for bringing me here. She has set out to do every goddamn little petty thing she can to make both you and me miserable."

"She is my daughter, Jim," Ria said evenly. "And I have to stick up for her in this matter. It has been hard for her, your

120

coming into our life. But you refuse to give her a chance. Yes, she's struck out at you. But no more than you've struck back at her. And, yes, she's struck out at me. But deep inside her is a very giving, very loving person. . . ."

I drained my glass and stood up, interrupting her mid-sentence.

"That's bullshit, Ria. And you know it."

Infuriated, I turned and walked out of the house. Before I had even reached my apartment, I had cooled down. Ria had not been all that off base, I knew, and it disturbed me that I had gotten so angry. As soon as I walked in the door of my apartment I called her and apologized. She thanked me for calling.

"Do you want to see me again?" I asked.

"Of course, darling," she said. "We just had our first little fight, that's all. Families do fight, you know. Now go on to bed. I love you. We'll get together this weekend. Tomorrow, Janet and I are going to have dinner, and I'm booked the next night. But, no, don't worry. Everything's fine."

But everything wasn't fine. At least, not with me. The mere mention of Janet's name and what a dear, sweet girl she was inside still set my blood boiling. And the remarks Ria had made about the Porsche had not set well either. Ria had indicated from our first lunch together that I was to be one of her heirs, which meant, by implication, a considerable sum of money. In that context, I hadn't regarded her "little gift," as she had described it, as my grubstake, the money with which I was to go to Wall Street and make my fortune.

And what if I had? What if Ria had made it as clear as well water that that fifteen grand was the sum total of my inheritance? I probably would've bought the Porsche anyway, as any psychiatrist in Beverly Hills could have told her. Although it annoyed me that Ria would give a gift and then carp about how I disposed of it, what really hurt was that she didn't understand why that car, that visible object, meant more to me than investment dividends, however hefty, ever could.

Ria and I got back together that weekend and everything seemed fine. She made no mention of our argument, nor did I.

121

All appeared to be going well until she learned that I had transferred from the city room at the *Times* to the View section.

I was excited about the move. I had tired of traveling all over
the United States, and there was a new city editor with whom
I'd been having conflicts. The move to View was exciting because
Jim Bellows, the talented former editor of the *New York Herald
Tribune,* was overseeing the View operation and wanted to make
the "lifestyle" section a showcase for *Times* writers. But to Ria,
the new job was a demotion that moved me off the prestigious
front page and into what she regarded as a far less important
section of the paper. Her attitude led me to believe that she was
more interested in prestige by association than she was in my
happiness as a writer.

With both of us so angry and critical, I should have sensed a
showdown in the near future. But I was too absorbed in my own
grievances to understand Ria's, so the blowup took me by surprise when, a few weeks later, it came. During one of the library
sessions in which both of us were fairly well down into the bottle,
Ria began enumerating all her complaints again—my unfriendli-
ness to Janet, my poor money management, my lack of interest
in her friends, my weight and the length of my beard—finally
concluding with a statement that first stung, then numbed me.

"I thought I was doing the right thing when I contacted you,
Jim. Now, I'm not so sure. I had no idea it was going to cause
so much pain and grief between Janet and me. I had no idea you
were so immature. To read your writing, one would think you
were very mature, very stable. But your actions have proven
otherwise. Throwing away that money I gave you, the horrible
way you behave in front of some of my friends, like the time you
just walked outside at Cynthia's party and didn't come back in
until I was so embarrassed I had to leave . . . all those things I
just never expected.

"Then there's your personal appearance. I spent a lot of
money buying you the right clothes to wear at the right places.
I taught you how to dress correctly and appropriately. But you
never keep your clothes cleaned and pressed, and you've let
yourself gain so much weight that none of them fit you anymore.

"And I cannot comprehend how you can act so childishly toward Janet. You are a lot older than she is and I would have thought you would certainly be able to act like an adult with her and understand that she would have a great deal harder time accepting you than you would accepting her."

Tears began to form in her eyes as she spoke. I sat staring at the floor.

"It's my fault," she said. "It's my own damn fault. I had this fairy tale picture of all of us being a real happy family. To be honest, I wish I had never written you that letter. It was a terrible mistake."

Her words fell into my consciousness like heavy stones. But the pain they caused was replaced by a burning anger. I very carefully poured myself a large drink and drained the glass. The whiskey burned down my throat, heating my anger.

"Let me tell you something, Ria. I want you to listen to every word I'm going to say. And I want you to remember these words." I stood up and walked over to where she was sitting. Standing over her, looking down at her, I began to speak.

"You know, that's pretty funny, the part about me being so damn immature. With the exception of a few men you know who are chairman of the board of some corporation or other, I am the only person in the entire bailiwick of your existence who has a job—who has to work, by God, for a living.

"And you know something else? You've been getting off on that! You enjoy the fact that I work, and you have also added one helluva lot of points to your own personal scoreboard by the fact that I am a writer, a journalist, a name that these people read, and whose work they admire.

"What did you have before I came along? A whimpering, bitchy little daughter, a jealous, conniving, selfish little twit who cannot stand the fact that her own goddamn brother has been able to start from the absolute bottom of the pile and work his way up to the top . . . all on his own, all without any help from any trust fund or anybody.

"Well, I'm tired of this shit. I'm tired of watching you swim in this endless fucking circle of the same boring people and the same boring restaurants where everyone wears the same boring clothes and has the same boring things to say.

"And yes, I have gained weight. Because you came on to me like gangbusters, lady. I've always had to fight my weight, and tell myself that it's good to deny yourself, good not to eat dessert or drink that second can of beer. Then you came along and told me school's out, all these no-no's are okay. You people do nothing but eat and drink all day and you don't get fat. Well, terrific. But don't act as if I'm a moral degenerate because I do.

"And yes, I spent that money. Because, goddammit, I never had any money to spend before. You bring me into a world of Rolls-Royces and expect me to want to buy a fucking Plymouth?"

My voice grew louder and louder. Ria shrank back in her chair as I loomed over her.

"As far as my behavior at your parties is concerned—well, it has taken a while for me to realize this, but I am my own man. I made myself. I raised myself. And once I was twenty-one and on my own, I never, until I met you, let anybody tell me what to do or force me to be with people I didn't want to be with. And it took a while for me to remember this. It took a while for me to remember that I don't like wearing suits and ties. And I don't like to be around people unless those people are doers, like me. And that, my dear, elegant, overstuffed and pathetic lady, is why I began to choose to walk outside and away from these droves of pretentious, coddled, do-nothing, know-nothing imitations of human beings.

"So now you say you made a mistake? No, Ria, I was the one who made the mistake. I got blinded by your fat jewels and your fat promises. I got blinded because I thought you were my mother who was finally coming to get me, finally coming to take me home where I thought, at long last, I finally belonged.

"But you're right. I don't belong. I don't belong here, and I don't belong anywhere except inside myself. As far as I'm concerned, Beverly Hills is just one big, steam-pressed, antiseptic cow patch, and you can keep it. It's all yours."

I turned and walked out of the room and out of the house. My mind was boiling, but even in my fury I could still see Ria, shrinking into her chair, her eyes wide with fear.

Chapter 8

This time there were no late-night, apologetic phone calls. I turned away from Ria and retreated into a world I thought I could control, dividing myself between the *Times,* where I worked, and my apartment, where I slept, drank wine, and watched television. But I could not stop thinking. The thoughts began to warp and collide, plunging me further into drunken delusion. Why had she done this to me? She had come to me and convinced me that money was more important than my work. What had I told myself when I transferred from city side to View? That I was joining a showcase for writers? Perhaps. But now I wondered if I had not changed slots to make it easier to fit into Ria's social schedule. View took me off the hard trail, where I was on call twenty-four hours a day, 365 days a year, and put me on an ordinary Monday-through-Friday routine. To be with her, I had given up one of the last jobs in journalism for insipid interviews with authors and actors who were dancing and prancing for recognition and dollars. And I had become one of them. I had danced and pranced just like them.

Finally it penetrated my brain. Finally I began to see it was all worse than nothing. She was just some Eve, holding out an apple.

I kept slipping away. I tried to make myself take long walks to keep away from the wine. But more and more, the walks were something I thought about doing. One morning I woke up in a lake of urine. I was still drunk. There was some woman lying in the urine with me. She was snoring. Her naked body was soaked and stinking, just like mine. Two empty gallon wine jugs lay on the floor. I looked at her and couldn't remember who she was, or how she'd gotten there. I went into the bathroom and vomited. The sound woke her up. She staggered into the bathroom and sat down on the floor and giggled while I retched into the toilet. Her craziness echoed off the tile walls until I became dizzy and began to lose consciousness. When I came to, she was gone. I was still on the bathroom floor. I managed to shower, clean up the mess in the bathroom, and haul the sheets down to the washing machine. I carried the mattress outside, washed it down with a hose, and laid it across the stucco stairs for the sun to dry. "I've got to stop this," I said to myself. Instead, I called in sick and went to the liquor store and bought two more gallons of wine.

The next morning I awoke in the same sea. This time I was alone. After cleaning up, I drank coffee and cooked a large breakfast. It was the first food I'd had in three days. When I knew it was going to stay down, I dressed and drove in to work. At lunch I asked a friend if she could recommend a good, common-sense psychologist. I knew now that unless I forced a change, my self-destructiveness was going to be the winner.

The psychologist had his offices in west Los Angeles. He agreed to see me that afternoon. When I took my seat in his conference room, I tried to ignore the fact he was wearing buckskin leggings, a buckskin shirt, moccasins, and beads around his neck. "Well, Jim," he said, smiling slightly. "Rachel said you appeared somewhat desperate. What seems to be wrong?"

"Doc," I said, as fervently as I could, "I just want to know one thing about myself. I want to know if I am going to be able to survive." For seven days I went to him. I talked, he listened. I told him as fast as I could the events of my childhood, the life

I had carved out for myself, the marriage to Theresa, and finally, the Ria story. Oddly, the more I talked, the more confident I grew. At home, I cut down on the drinking. I stopped thinking the painful thoughts that I had poured so much wine down my throat to dull. Then I began to tire of talking. On the seventh day I went to him and said, "Well, what about it? Can I?"

He looked at me for a time. "Yes, you will survive," he finally said. "I've never seen anyone more determined to survive."

It was as if I had a new lease on a new life. I quit drinking entirely. I went on a high-protein diet and cut back from four packs of cigarettes a day to one. Every day after work I would ride my bike to one of the steep canyon roads and pump straight up. My writing went well.

One evening, somewhat ceremoniously, I took all the clothing Ria had purchased for me and stored it in a closet I never used. I bought new workshirts and jeans and comfortable, soft-soled shoes. I wore this uniform to work, and I wore it when I began dining out again in the neighborhood restaurants. I wasn't up to serious dating; instead I got to know a few local types; one skipped an anchovy boat, another was a part-time actor who owned an interest in Alice's Restaurant, the place where I came to hang out. It was a neutral time, a time for me to think about what I was going to do with my life.

One thing seemed to become clearer with each passing day: I needed very much to know the truth of how I had come to be. While there was no question Ria was my biological mother, there were some big questions in my mind about how she had come to play that role. In my sobriety, I had been reviewing the things she had told me, and I kept stumbling over contradictions, mostly concerning her attitude toward my father. Furthermore, the very drama of her account made me suspicious. It was such a typical Ria story. I couldn't doubt the substance, but I couldn't trust her interpretations. And the interpretations really mattered.

It was time, I decided, to go back to my other mother. I was sure that Edith could shed some light. And I was sure she would. Because I was determined that if she resisted I would force her, by whatever means, to spill it out. She owed me. She couldn't heal the hurts her coldness had inflicted, but she could tell me the truth about me. That was one debt she was not going to have a choice about paying.

Meadowbrooke, North Carolina, seemed a million years away from Los Angeles that October—1974—when I drove the rental car across the city line. I found it difficult to believe I'd been raised in this town, or had come back there to be married. It was as if I had lived many lives and this place was two lives behind me. I drove down North Street, where years before I had walked a policeman's beat. The scene was much the same—fewer businesses, perhaps, and a few more bars. I drove to the old high school and parked beside the football field, trying to imagine the feel of cleats digging into the dirt, the thunk of body contact, the yelling of the crowd. There was nothing there. No memories. No feelings.

I had an hour before sundown. I drove back out of town to the cemetery. I parked and walked across the grass, this time straight to my father's grave. Kneeling down beside the bronze plaque, I closed my eyes and tried once more to bring back some sense of him. Once again the memories were not there. I sat down on the grass and lit a cigarette, staring at his name. A few things fluttered in my mind, but they were too faint to grasp.

I stared hard at the plaque. Had I been making all this up . . . my feelings for him, the bond we shared? I lit another cigarette, gazed down at the bronze plaque for a long moment, and then slowly got up from the grass.

When I reached home, the sun had dipped behind the pines along the river's western shore. The bay was a sheet of glass, flawed here and there by the splashes of jumping mullet. It was low tide and the stench of the exposed, brackish mud filled the autumn air. A light was burning inside the house and my mother's Plymouth was parked under the carport. I sat in the car awhile, trying to think how to tell her what I knew.

I had always had a problem telling her anything. It was her bearing, mostly. She was typical of a people that inhabited that part of North Carolina called the Green Swamp. It was a land of ignorance, of stubbornness, of secretiveness, a refuge for moonshiners, escaped prisoners and poachers, for alligators, cottonmouth moccasins, and mean-jawed snapping turtles. Edith had shaped her whole life, her thoughts, her goals, her manners, so no one would ever guess she'd come from there. Her bearing was her armor. And her armor was like drop-forged steel.

I went to the back door and knocked, and she came out in an old, ragged housecoat. "Come on in," she said. "I didn't know if you were coming in tonight or tomorrow, and it was getting so late. I just went ahead on to bed." We hugged each other woodenly and I told her to go back to bed, that I'd see her in the morning.

The next morning I woke at dawn and went down the stairs to the kitchen. The kitchen smelled of stale food. The house smelled stale too, as if the doors hadn't been opened in years. I opened the refrigerator, and it was full of moldy jars and other items that I could not readily identify. I crept outside and drove to a restaurant for breakfast.

When I returned, she was up, but still dressed in the old robe. She wore it the entire day. We sat and talked, but the talk was from her, and mostly about who had died and how much she still felt hurt by my divorce. She kept on talking, sometimes repeating herself several times over. She had become old, I thought. It was only three years since I'd seen her, but in that time she had become an old woman. The house smelled of her oldness. But she seemed as happy as one could expect. She spoke with pride about my journalistic accomplishments, making it clear, however, that she was surprised by it all.

The more I listened, the more a voice inside of me said, *Let it be, man.* She was old. What good was it going to do to bring back this thing on her? It was too late, anyway. Confronting her wasn't going to change a damn thing. It wasn't going to bring back my childhood or close the wounds. So what if I never would know what really happened? What real difference was that going to make? The only sure thing was that it would cause her pain. She was content in her mind that I was her son. All of her friends complimented her on how well I'd done. Why disturb that? Why mess it up for her? She was old, and alone, and her son was really all she had left.

I stayed two more days. There were moments when I almost began to say it. But then I would look at her, and that voice would come back, and I would shake my head and look the other way, talk of something else. I felt good inside about it. I had spared her what she had not spared me, and I was good for having done that. I had been considerate and forgiving. The matter, I told myself, was closed.

When I had planned the trip to confront Edith, I had figured on a traumatic time. In anticipation of that, I had arranged two weeks leave from the *Times*, guessing most of the first week would be spent dealing with Edith and scheduling a week in New Orleans and Acapulco afterward, to give me time to cool off in a neutral zone. Now I decided to take the vacation anyway. I drove from Meadowbrooke to Raleigh, still buoyed by my feeling of benevolence, and boarded a jet to New Orleans. But as the plane lifted off and North Carolina passed below, a gnawing feeling of frustration again began to spread within me. I ordered a double vodka and let the liquor, the first I'd had in many months, sweetly burn the frustration away. I began to relax, to anticipate how good the trip was going to be.

In Los Angeles, I had read and dreamed of New Orleans— Cajuns, Creoles, dusky women with dancing devil eyes, the boundless street-born jazz of the black men who celebrated even death as life. But as I lay on my king-size bed at the Royal Orleans Hotel, listening to the sounds of laughing couples on the street below, I felt very tired.

The only images that came were those of my father's grave, of the old woman, Edith, how shrunken and withered she seemed, so final in her nothingness. And there was again the image of Ria, huddled in that chair, her body trembling, her eyes wide with fear.

I flew on to Acapulco and checked into Las Brisas, a colony of expensive bungalows spread up a mountainside overlooking the bay. I had a private swimming pool and a refrigerator stocked with good Mexican beer. I also had myself. And I wasn't sure what to do with that. I thumbed through the resort's brochure and decided to charter a deep-sea fishing boat the next morning.

The sea had a good chop that day. A wind raked across the waves, making them burst into spray. The skipper of the vessel, a pudgy Mexican with a permanent smile, told the mate, a solemn Indian, to rig baits from the outriggers. The scudding sea made it nearly impossible for me to keep my eyes on the trailing, skipping baits. My mind drifted, lulled by the motion of the boat and the water.

I had congratulated myself that my war with Edith was over, the case was closed. But I had been a fool to think so. Everything led back to Edith. I had fought Edith all the way, yet today I was the man she'd made me, and a lot of people, including me, had suffered for it. I was a man who stole from every woman he ever met, and did so with a sense of righteousness.

I was scared. I felt very close to the heart of things. I knew that I'd been wrong to leave her there intact, to hide the anger, hide the pain that was searing me, suppress the questions that were driving me crazy. My life was nearly half over. Unless I went back to Edith, the second half would be a repeat of the first. Without ever knowing I was a bastard by birth, I had felt myself a bastard in life—never acceptable, always isolated from the legitimate ones. I was determined that would change. I felt my shell splintering. I wanted to say, without thinking less of myself, "I need." And I wanted to be able to give when someone else asked.

*"Señor! Señor!"*

I was jerked from my thoughts as the captain yelled down from the bridge. I saw the mate grab one of the two thick, stubby deck rods and whip it back over his shoulder, once, twice. A large black form boiled out of the ocean far behind the wake of the boat and thrashed the blue air with his stiletto-tipped head. A sailfish. Flashes of color came from his dorsal fin as he crashed back into the sea.

The mate thrust the pole into my hands at the moment the fish hit the water, and the reel's drag sang as the creature sounded. I tightened down the drag, only to have the line go slack. Quickly

I reeled in. The water exploded as the fish jumped again, his huge body writhing, his great head frantically trying to shake the barbed steel lose from his jaw. I played him for what seemed like an hour. Finally I was able to bring him close to the boat. When the fish was alongside, the Indian mate grasped the fish by his bill and pulled him halfway out of the sea, exposed for me to see. His colors were brilliant, his fin like some war flag of Neptune.

I set the pole down and stumbled from my chair. The captain was smiling. I smiled back at him, got my Nikon from a bag, and clicked off a roll of film. I was reloading when I saw the Indian begin dragging the exhausted fish into the boat.

"No," I told the captain. "Let him go."

The smile disappeared from the captain's face. "But, *señor,* he is a trophy! You do not want him for your wall?"

"He's not my trophy," I told him. "He doesn't belong on a wall. He belongs in the sea. Let him go."

From behind me I heard a "thunk!" and turned to see the Indian standing over the fish with a large, hardwood club. The fish quivered and died.

"Take me back to shore," I told the captain, furious and sad. The captain shrugged and went back up on the bridge, restarted the engines, and turned the craft toward the bay. The Indian strapped the big fish across the stern. When we reached the Las Brisas dock, I gathered the few things I had brought out with me and prepared to step ashore. I took one last look at the dead fish. I thought of my father's ashtray.

Chapter 9

Although I couldn't have said why, my journey back to Los Angeles, via New Orleans and Acapulco, also brought me back to Ria. In the time and distance that had separated us, I had realized that I did not want to be estranged from her, that her heart was kind and generous, her impulses well-intended. Things had gone awry, but not because she'd meant me any harm.

Ria received me cautiously. It was clear that she was still stinging from my denunciations. But, in the manner of two friends who really do not wish to be enemies, we let the subject drop, and our relationship slowly resumed. She had, after all, given birth to me. I was her son. What else mattered?

My professional life took a turn at this point. In November 1974, I became a contributing editor for *True,* a men's magazine that had been a big success in the pre-Hefner days of Hemingway-Ruark values. It had just been purchased by Petersen Publishing Company in Los Angeles. The new executive publisher hired me, at one thousand dollars per month, to help see if it could be revitalized.

The income, added to my *Times* salary, put me in such good

stead that in December I moved to a one-bedroom beachfront apartment on Old Malibu Road. Ria was pleased by my apparent capitulation to capitalism, materialism, and status—my neighbors included Shirley MacLaine, Norman Fell, David Carradine, and other "names"—and she gave me an apartment-warming gift. I was pleased, too. The highway sounds that had plagued my previous apartment were replaced by the sound of the winter ocean slapping the sands of my front yard. I arranged my work table in the alcove that looked out over the sea. I bought a pair of binoculars and spent hours scanning the ocean, remembering the old river pilots who would tirelessly search the waves off North Carolina's Frying Pan Shoals for ships to guide up the Cape Fear River. Sometimes I would catch a herd of spouting, diving gray whales, heading to Baja, or a flight line of pelicans flapping lazily toward Point Dume.

Come spring and summer, I knew, the beach would be thronged by young women on parade, hoping to catch the eye of one of the producers, directors, and actors who lived along the shorefront. But this was winter, and the beach belonged to sea birds and hooded joggers. The only others were the fishermen, warmly dressed figures with light surf fishing tackle who seemed too businesslike to be sportsmen. Curious, I walked out one day and examined them more closely. They would walk to a jetty, break off some of the mussels that grew in clusters there, and then bait their hooks with mussel meat and cast their lines just beyond the breakers. Soon would come glittering, silver catches of perch, which they silently packed away until their bags were full. Then they would be gone. I learned they were all from Little Japan, in downtown Los Angeles.

But the best of all winter diversions in Malibu was Alice's Restaurant, a lovely retreat on the near end of Malibu Pier. I went each afternoon, when my work was done and before the dinner crowds began their surge, to enjoy the wood and plants and windows facing the sea. Soon it was as much a part of my life as anything had ever been. As I took my place at the bar, a double shot of gold tequila would be placed in front of me, along with a cup of coffee.

Except for a greeting by Bob Yuro, the actor who was part-owner of the restaurant, or a hello from Dennis the chef, I was left to myself there. Now that I was writing for View, a lot of people thought nothing of badgering me in public for coverage of their clients, or themselves, and the unfailing reticence of Alice's patrons was a great relief. Even movie stars could hide out there, and some, like Steve McQueen, Ali MacGraw, and Kris Kristofferson, did so regularly. Something about Alice's seemed to preclude hardcore star-gazing and autograph hounding.

That was Malibu. Status was not acknowledged overtly. Knowns mingled with unknowns at the pharmacy, the grocery store, and on the beach. I might find myself bumping shopping carts with Burt Lancaster or standing beside Cary Grant and his little girl at the medical clinic. You never knew.

Needless to say, life in Beverly Hills paled by comparison. What had once seemed like a dream world of self-indulgence now seemed stifling and pretentious. What seemed even sillier to me was that while Ria and her friends were all so rich, they wouldn't allow themselves to be comfortable. For each outing, Ria and I had to wear the correct uniform. Scuffs on shoes had to be burnished away, wrinkles had to be ironed. My neck began to choke from the ties I had to wear. Instead of being freed by their money, these people had let it enmesh them.

But the more serious problem between Ria and me continued to be Janet. She had broken up with Ronald, and Ria was predicting that that would mean the end of the cold war between Janet and me. "Things will be better now," she said. "You'll see."

I didn't like Ria campaigning for Janet, and I liked even less being told that she was simultaneously campaigning with Janet for me. By this time, however, I was determined not to make waves, so I played along, which was more than Janet was willing to do. She met Ria's sales job with a sublime lack of interest. This disturbed Ria greatly. She expected me to sympathize in the matter, which I did not, and pleaded for me to understand Janet's plight, which I did. Janet and I had the same problem—

we hated each other. If one of us was winning the war, it was Janet. The more hostile she became, the more time Ria devoted to wooing her.

One weekend in November, Ria and I went down to Palm Springs together. It was the first time in many months that she and I had spent more than just a few hours together. The Palm Springs house, which Ria had inherited from Dave, was large and opulent and located in an exclusive compound with a uniformed guard posted at the entrance. "The winter place," Ria called it. I liked to sit under a grapefruit tree in the backyard and sip wine while watching workmen, not far away, building Bob Hope's new home. When we lunched at the Racquet Club that first day, George Burns dropped by the table to say hello. The next morning, on a liquor run to downtown Palm Springs, I saw Red Skelton, who was carrying a heavy leather satchel, puffing on a giant cigar, and smiling and greeting everyone, including me, as if we were all one big family. But the fascination began to wear thin.

As on my last visit, everything was scheduled—breakfast with the So-and-So's, lunch here, cocktails there, and dinner somewhere else; everything was determined—where we went, what we wore, how long we were to stay. I grinned and bore it. This was the lifestyle gap between Ria and me, and I was determined not to let it divide us. I had myself under control until one evening at still another deadly cocktail party. I had been cornered by a seventy-five-year-old Harvard lad who was regaling me with his accounts of his collegiate feats and, worse, his latest jokes, and I found myself slowly but steadily slipping into the same mental state in which I had last ripped into Ria. At a moment when no one was watching, I ducked out the back door, climbed into Ria's Rolls and, with the lights out, stole away from the house. I flipped the lights on at a safe distance, gave a good smile to the guard at the gate, and turned right on the highway, heading for downtown Palm Springs.

Like Beverly Hills, Palm Springs shuts down at sunset except for the restaurants and saloons. I bypassed the fancy places, knowing what sort of people I would find inside, and started checking out the other, humbler spots, looking for people of my own age. My luck was less than good. It was a week night. On weekends, the town filled with young women from Los Angeles. But this was Tuesday. At midnight, after two fruitless hours of searching, I gave up and pulled into a small pizza joint for a beer. The waitress was a woman in her late thirties. She looked tired, but there was sparkle in her eye.

"Honey, don't spend too much time on that beer," she said. "We gotta close this joint down now."

I looked at the other waitress, who was about the same age. The two were obviously buddies, and a thought began to tickle my mind. "What are you two ladies going to do after work?" I asked the first one.

"What we do every night, honey. Go home, fix a drink, and rest our barking dogs."

"Well," I told her, "I have this problem. I'm here from L.A., and I'm staying with the most boring group of people I've ever known in my life. What would you two say to joining me for a late dinner, a few drinks, and maybe even a laugh or two? It just might save my sanity." She walked over to the other woman, whispered in her ear, and looked back at me. She grinned, nodded, and twenty minutes later the three of us were headed out of Palm Springs to a late-night restaurant.

"Goddamn," said the first woman, Cheryl, leaning back in the front seat, "first time I've ever ridden in a Rolls-Royce."

"Yes, honey!" came Pauline's voice from the back. "We're finally going first class!"

Both women had changed clothes at the pizza place and were wearing slacks, blouses, and low-heeled shoes.

By 2:00 A.M. we were quite drunk, full of good, nongourmet food, and back on the road again, this time with two bottles of tequila I'd purchased from the bartender. We drove out into the desert, following a winding, sand-covered, two-lane road. We turned off onto an even smaller road, pulled to a stop, and got out of the car, leaving the radio on and tuned in to a pop music station. With me in the middle, the three of us danced—staggered—and giggled until we finally fell into a heap on the sand.

138

Cheryl decided she wanted to do a strip for our benefit. She staggered to her feet and, swaying almost in time to the music, began taking off all her clothes. Pauline, who had a rather remarkable figure, managed to rise and divest herself of her garments as well. The last thing I remember was two blurry, naked images coming toward me. . . .

The desert sun had just begun its climb into the eastern sky when I woke up and painfully tried to focus my eyes. All I could see was gray. I blinked several times and finally realized I was staring at the upholstered roof of the Rolls. I sat up, wincing, and looked over the back of the seat. The two women, still nude, were snoring gently—one on the seat and the other on the floorboard. An hour later I had dropped them off at their apartment in Palm Springs, and it was 7:00 A.M. when I rolled into Ria's driveway. Moving as quietly as I could, I entered by the side door and went to my room where I lay across the bed and quickly fell asleep.

At 9:00 A.M. I woke up and, after washing my face and combing my hair, made my way to the kitchen. Ria was sitting alone at the table, drinking coffee and reading the morning paper. I poured myself a cup and sat down at the table, smiling crookedly.

The smile was not returned.

"I did not tell you you could take my car last night, Jim," she said, her eyes cold and angry. "And I most certainly did not expect you to be gone all goddamn night with it and then return it with sand all over the seats and floors and with the interior reeking of cheap perfume and booze! And God only knows what else!"

Her words, pitched higher and tighter than normal, pierced my head like twenty-penny nails. I tried to develop a civil, apologetic answer but failed. "I just got bored last night," I said. "For three days and three nights I've been surrounded with this bunch of old toots, and it finally got to me. I didn't think you'd mind my taking a break."

"Those old toots are my friends, darling," she replied. "And that car that you took who knows where is an $80,000 investment that I happen to prize very much." She went on and on, but the point was made. I knew I had screwed up and I knew I had done it intentionally. But I didn't know why.

There was little said between us the rest of that day. When the sun finally set and the desert began to cool, I took a long walk alone, trying to get myself straight about what had happened. I'd been thoughtless and inconsiderate, but the truth was, I had been much happier with the two pizza ladies than I had been the entire time in Palm Springs with Ria. I fought this feeling, and returned to the house where another cocktail party was well under way. I fortified myself with three quick drinks and managed to be as charming and pleasant as anyone there. Ria noticed and gave me a hug. But she kept her eye on me—and her car—the entire evening.

Back in Los Angeles, Ria and I continued to see each other when she could schedule around Janet. But something had changed between us. And this time, there seemed a permanence to the change. Ria obviously felt that I was the cause of her problems with Janet, and she would never let anything come between her and her daughter. Toward her son, her feelings were not quite so clear.

For a long time I had been weary of Ria's obsession with telling me "our" story. Much more interesting, at this point, was the story of Ria's life after my birth. How had this "poor, little backwoods girl" arrived at such prominence in a place where prominence was not easily achieved, nor easily maintained over a long period of time? Her name appeared almost daily in Jody Jacobs's society column. Her charity work stood alongside that of the most prominent names in Los Angeles. Her home often served as a receiving center for foreign royalty. More than once I had bumped into a Lord and Lady Somebody as they strolled through the rose garden.

But when I was with Ria, alone, the subject was always the same. And she began to add even more variations. Not only had my father raped her, not only had she nearly died in childbirth, now she was saying that my mother forged the Stingley name on the birth certificate.

These new revelations always came after drinks, usually late at night in her library.

"So you see, Jim, I could never be your mother now. I never was. I was never allowed to be. You were taken from me. Even though I had almost died having you!"

When we were alone, this was her constant theme. But, oddly enough, when we were dining out, either alone or in the company of her friends, she would change course and talk on and on about how much the two of us were physically alike. She would tug at my red beard and say, "You got that from Big Red, my father." If I grew silent during a long social affair, she would chide me, saying, "Uh-huh! Just like Grandfather Stafford. Old solemn face!"

It was beginning to rip up my insides. In one mood, I was the spitting image of her, the carrier of her father's and his father's genes. In another, I wasn't her child at all, only the memento of a rape, a child who had nearly killed her in her womb and then vanished from her life. Janet was family, I was a bad dream.

Why was she yanking me around like this? Was I her son or not? Why was her daughter's ego more important than our entire relationship? And if I was, indeed, only on the fringes of the family, why did she sometimes go on and on about the bloodlines we shared?

This time I pulled away without a scene. Gradually, I secluded myself. I tried very hard to wash her words from my mind. But that was the trouble. The more she had said, the more her version of "our" story hadn't washed. And the more I thought about that, the more I knew that there was only one person on this earth who could shed any light at all on what I'd been told. I didn't want to go to her; had not been able to confront her. But now I began to wonder; how much longer could I go on with all this wrenching around inside of me? How much longer could I say it didn't matter?

Now, when I was not working, I spent many of my hours standing in the wet line of the winter surf, casting my hook in the churning waters that rolled just behind the wave break, trying to let the sound of the ocean drown out my thoughts. I didn't know if it would work, but I had my father's example to follow. He had always loved fishing, and now I felt that perhaps I knew the reason. He seemed to have had a lot to drown out himself.

Inside the apartment, I would sit at my work desk in the alcove, the telephone a reach away. I do not remember how many times I took the receiver from its cradle, held it to my ear, then slowly set it down again, as the picture of the old woman in her old robe materialized and my old excuse whispered inside my head. A part of me was still fighting, still saying that the matter was best left alone, that the old woman in Meadowbrooke had nothing left in life but this lie that she had come to see as reality.

But there now was emerging another part of me. And its voice was one I had never heard inside myself before.

*What about you?* it said. *When you asked the psychologist if you could survive, were you serious? Because if you were, you're sure blowing it now. You're close to blowing apart.*

*Hard, isn't it. The* Times *can't protect you now. This isn't a story that you can run with hard, then drop on the editor's desk and walk away. This isn't San Quentin or Attica. You can't hop a plane and get away from this to the safety of your cubbyhole at the paper or the privacy of your apartment with no number on the door, no name on the mailbox, no listed phone.*

*And what is really terrifying you is that you can't stand the truth that keeps hitting you between the eyes. You are so afraid . . . of what? That Ria is lying? Or that Ria is telling the truth?*

*What hurts the worst? Having been sucked in? Or having been told a tale that shatters the only belief you've ever tried to hold in your heart—that, apart from all of his faults and troubles, your father was a decent, good man?*

*Unless you face what's hurting, you're going to destroy yourself. And you are destroying yourself. . . .*

The voice stayed. No matter what I did, it stayed. For seven straight nights I tried my best to drink it away, but the next morning, it was there again. On the last of those nights I had dinner out with Ria. As usual, after several drinks, she began the tale again. My hands shook as she talked, but she never noticed. She had a way of becoming so absorbed in her own telling that it was as though she were on a stage, blinded by the lights, speaking her lines to an audience that was unseen, lost in the power of her performance.

I didn't interrupt her. I wouldn't have known what to say. Instead I gulped down glass after glass of pure vodka and went home later with the voice still raging inside me. That night I had a dream. In the dream I was screaming into a telephone. But the telephone had no cord. Next I was pounding on the door of my home in Meadowbrooke. But the door was opened by a woman I'd never seen before, who told me I had the wrong address, that she'd never heard of the person I was looking for.

I awoke at dawn, showered, and dressed. The alcohol of the night before had burned itself clean from my body, leaving my mind clear for the first time in seven days. Even the voice was silent.

I drove to Santa Monica and had breakfast, reading the *Times*. I drove to the office, checked the mail, spoke with my editor about several assignments, and then drove back to Malibu.

It was 1:00 P.M. Pacific Standard Time. In Meadowbrooke, North Carolina, it was four. I poured a mug of coffee and walked to the desk in the alcove. I lit a cigarette and picked up the telephone.

Chapter 10

The day I was to pick up Edith at the Greyhound depot in downtown Los Angeles it was cold and foggy in Malibu. Being Edith, she had refused to fly, even though I had offered to pay her way first class. Flying was too expensive, she said. Besides that, she had never done it and, despite the urgency of my appeal that she visit me as soon as possible, she was not going to start flying now. The very thought of it scared her to pieces, she said. Then, too, there were friends and relatives she wanted to visit in Texas and Arkansas on her return trip. By scheduling her visits properly, she could take advantage of the bus line's special excursion rate which, she pointed out, would save money while at the same time allowing her to spend some extra time in California, visiting Theresa and her family.

I had not argued with her. The important thing was that she was coming, and that she had promised to sit down with me, for however long it took, and tell me what I had told her I had to know.

I had let the phone ring nine or ten times, that day, and had

144

been on the verge of hanging up when she finally picked up the receiver.

"Hello?" she'd said.

"Mama?"

"Oh, Jimmy, it's you. I was outside working on the carport and almost didn't hear the phone ring. I'm trying to get some more of those old bricks laid down, plus a million other things that need to be done in the backyard. Old what's-his-name was supposed to come help me today, but he hasn't got here yet. Of course he's so old and pokey it's almost like not having any help at all. But he tries, and you know, Jimmy, you just can't get anybody to do any yard work for you anymore. . . ."

"Mama—"

"And the boathouse is about to fall into the canal. I just don't know what I'm going to do about that. The water keeps eating the bank away under it. But I'm just going to have to let it go until I get the leaks fixed on the front porch. . . ."

"Mama. I got this letter from this woman, Mama, and she says she's my mother."

"I . . ." Her voice trailed off, and there was silence for what seemed an interminable time. When she spoke again, it was in a tone I'd never heard her use before—soft and resigned.

"I knew that was going to happen, Jimmy. I prayed that it never would, but I knew I was fooling myself. Somehow I knew you were going to find out."

"Mama. I need to know what happened. I need for you to come out here and sit down with me and tell me. I'll pay your way. It won't cost you a cent. But I have got to know, Mama. And you've got to come here and tell me. Mama? You hear me?"

"Yes, Jimmy. Yes. I'll come. I'll come."

"You owe it to me, Mama."

"Yes, honey, I know. I know. I owe it to you."

The rest of the conversation was given to the business of how and when she would get to Los Angeles. When that was done, I told her I loved her and that I would be waiting for her arrival. When I placed the receiver back in its cradle, I rested my forehead on the tips of my fingers, letting my thumbs catch my cheekbones, I finally breathed.

She hadn't asked who or when or anything. She had shown no surprise, voiced no objection, expressed no sorrow. Strangely enough, it seemed almost as if something inside her had been waiting for that call for many, many years.

The Greyhound depot in downtown Los Angeles is not the classiest place the city has to offer. It's a hangout for pimps waiting for the latest little girl runaway to fall into their laps. It has the smell of people needing baths and the look of perma-drab. It's a place where luggage comes with twine tied around it and old people walk aimlessly or sit vacantly, clutching wrin-kled shopping bags that haven't been used for shopping in a long time. I arrived there on time, knowing the bus wouldn't. I parked, went inside to get an estimated time of arrival, and then returned to my car to wait. Edith's bus pulled in an hour later. I stood on the passenger dock, watching for her tiny, old body to take the tentative steps down to the concrete.

I almost didn't recognize her. She'd had her hair dyed blond and "done" into a rather smart style. She wore a suit that was new, flattering, and perhaps expensive. I hadn't seen her look so well in years. I walked up to the bus door and helped her down the steps, taking a piece of hand luggage from her. We hugged, but almost perfunctorily. She was visibly nervous and spoke only when she asked me to retrieve her luggage. At all times she avoided my eyes.

On the long, silent drive to Malibu, she positioned herself rigidly in the seat beside me, never looking anywhere but straight ahead. Only once, when we stopped at a red light, did our eyes meet. I had never seen an expression like that in the eyes of anyone. It was a mixture of great, nearly haughty pride, and genuine fear.

When I guided her into my apartment, she paused, looking around with apparent interest, and then sat down in a cushioned chair that faced the sea. I lit the fire, then sat down on the couch, turning so that we faced each other.

146

"Look, Mama, I know you've had a long haul, and you're probably worn out. We could start this tomorrow. . . ."

"No, Jimmy. No. I don't want to wait until tomorrow," she said, reaching into her purse. She pulled out a tissue and blew her nose.

"You know, Mama, you and I never did have much to say to each other," I said, moving beside her and putting my hand on her shoulder.

"I know it, Jimmy," she said, looking away from me. "I'm not an outgoing person, and I wish . . ." She paused, wiping her eyes with the tissue. "Jimmy," she said, in the same soft tone she'd used that day on the telephone, "fix me a drink."

I went to the bar and fixed drinks for both of us. Then I crossed the living room to the alcove where my desk was. I returned to the couch with my tape recorder and a stack of ninety-minute cassettes and placed them on the driftwood coffee table in front of me.

"What is that?" she asked.

"A tape recorder, Mama."

"Oh, I don't want to be on any tape recorder, Jimmy."

"I need a record of this, Mama. It is very important to me that I have every word you say here on tape."

She eyed the Sony TC-45. "It makes me nervous."

I took the tape recorder off the table and placed it on the couch by my side, where she couldn't see it. I unwrapped a new cassette and inserted it, then pushed the red RECORD button down and START lever forward.

"Just don't pay any attention to it, Mama," I said. "Just pretend it isn't there."

"I don't know, Jimmy. It reminds me of Watergate, or one of those kind of somethings."

"Well, it's not Watergate, and I'm not Nixon." I smiled. "Look, Mama," I said, changing the subject and the tone of my voice, falling unconsciously into a simple, homely pattern of speech, "there's some things you have to understand about me now. I really respect you. I have for a long time. I didn't when I was a kid because, well, I just didn't know a lot of things to respect you for when I was trying so hard to be understood myself. You just weren't able to do that, you know, you did the best you could. And I appreciate that more than you know. I appreciate it for a lot of different reasons.

"Now something has happened to me. And I have been going through a very hard, hard time the last two years. I debated and debated on whether even to tell you about it. Because at first I thought, well, there's nothing to be settled by telling you. And then . . . then I found out that there *is* something to be settled— just to get my own head cleared. Okay? And you and I . . . in my own way, Mama, I love you . . . but I can't . . . you know, it's hard for me to show that, because of the way it all was with you and me.

"But, Mama, I had a woman come to me and tell me she was my real mother."

"Yes, Jimmy."

"Now that means she born me. Don't mean a damn thing else, okay? And it made me love you even more . . . much more . . . it really did! I was really proud of you then, because, like I told her, now I understand a lot of things.

"But she had a lot of guilt hanging over her head . . . a lot of guilt. And I told her that there was nothing to worry about because people are only human beings, okay?"

"Yes."

"But for two years, Mama . . . that's what I went back to North Carolina to tell you. But then I thought, what good would it do? I didn't want to hurt you. But then later on I thought, well, she's a strong lady, she can handle it, she can help you with it. So, Mama, you don't know what a relief it is to be able to tell you this because . . ."

"Oh, you don't know how I have worried over the years, Jimmy. And everything that would happen to you . . . when you were disturbed and things like that . . . I thought, well, it was retribution. Because I had done something that was wrong, and I was being punished. And you know I don't let you know how much it hurts me when things don't go right with you."

"I know how you keep it inside of yourself, Mama," I said. "I

148

know that. You've told me a lot of times that you couldn't show feelings, and I've always been the guy who showed everything. But for two years, Mama, I've kept that inside me. Until last week when I couldn't . . . I just couldn't do it another day."

"Well, I'm glad that you . . ."

"I had to tell you, Mama, because I want to ask you what happened. In her version there's a lot of blank spaces because she's blocked it out entirely. Now, she respects you and she admires you and even when she came to me, Mama, she said, 'Now, listen, I am not your mother. I just gave birth to you.' That's what she told me. But she said she had to tell me. She just had to. She actually . . . Mama, I think she needed me at that point."

"I had lost touch with her entirely, Jimmy, and didn't know where . . . and I blocked her out too, you see, because . . ."

"But you don't need to block it out, Mama. Because it is all right. And because it is very important to me to know who I am and why it happened. I've been wondering who I am all my life, Mama. All my life! And if you can tell me . . ."

"Well, Jimmy, actually it was my fault and never would have happened, if I . . ."

She stopped talking and took a long sip from her drink. I could hear the sound of the waves breaking outside and my own ragged breathing. But I had to keep her going.

"What, Mama?"

"Jimmy, everybody—every woman—would like to have children by her husband. But I had a tumor. And I had to have my uterus removed. So I could have no children. And so I thought, well, if I couldn't have any children, there'd be no reason why, if somebody would be willing, if we knew somebody or something like that, then I could have Jim's child just the same, you see. At that time, 'Mama'—your grandmother—was not well at all. So I started looking around for somebody that could maybe stay with her and we could get to know each other. Of course, Mama didn't know anything about it. Nobody does. And Roy was not too happy about it. Oh, I'm the one, really and truly, I'm the one, Jimmy.

"Anyway, you see, Roy was working for the U.S. Forest Service and we got to go a lot of places . . . and we got to know this girl. And she came and stayed with us. And we got to be real good friends."

"How did you meet her?" I said.

"Let me see . . . I believe that, I can't remember whether we met her at some dance or some little something that we went to."

"Where?"

"That was back in eastern North Carolina, down in Wade County. She had come from a good family, but, you know, times were hard then, and so I told her about my mother needing someone to care for her. And she came and stayed with us awhile.

"We never did go down to Mama's. We lived in Old Pine. So then . . . now, she had ambition and wanted to be something and so . . . let me see now, was that before or after . . . ? Now Jimmy, this sounds terrible, but I have tried to block it out of my mind, as though it never happened."

I looked at her. Tears were welling in her eyes. "But now you don't have to, Mama."

"Well, but I still do. Because I feel I made an awful mistake, Jimmy. I was playing God. See?"

"That's okay, Mama. That's okay. It all worked out okay."

She dabbed at her eyes and took another drink.

"So then . . . we went up to Virginia—I had these friends there. And so when she was pregnant we went up there. And then I had friends in West Virginia, and that was one reason I did a lot of going during that time. Everybody thought you were my natural child, you see, because I had always been gadabouting up there. And there we sent her to take a beauty school course in Raleigh . . . she was just a lovely girl. . . ."

"But this was after I was born?"

"Yes."

"I want to back up some, Mama. Now how did it happen that she came in with you? Didn't she have a family?"

"Her mother was dead. Her father was married again, but I don't think he was much."

"Did Daddy know her father?"

"He'd met him."

"Did they go fishing together?"

"I don't think so, but Roy knew him."

"Did Dad know her initially?"

"No, I'm the one who met her initially. But, Jimmy, Roy was not for the idea."

"But you told him about it. How did you approach him? What did you say?"

"I don't remember. I was so upset back then. But he wasn't going to go along with it."

"But you met her, you brought her in the house, and you told him that you would like to have a child by her?"

"Yes. And he went along with it. He had respect for her and all that. He was not in love with her or anything like that. . . ."

She paused again, the tears now gone. "In a way," she said, "it meant something to her to have the influence. We were, you know, from a different background, and it could help her. Because she did so very, very well."

"Mama, did you make a deal with her?"

"No. No, it just sort of fell into place."

"You mean he just one night went into her room and . . ."

"Yes, it just came about."

"How did you handle the pregnancy aspect of it?"

"Well, that wasn't a great something or other, because she was a big girl, and she didn't show right away, and so, then, she went on to beauty school, you see. . . ."

"How long did it take to get her pregnant, Mama?"

"About two months or three months. Something like that. I forget if we sent her to beauty school first, or what, and then she came back. She wasn't there with us all the time. But it did take several months. We were friends. . . ."

"How old was she?"

"Eighteen or nineteen. About nineteen years old."

"Had she graduated from high school?"

"No. No. And I helped her a lot because she had only been to about the seventh grade. But she had a good native intelligence. . . . I knew she lived in California, Jimmy. I've thought about that several times, fearing . . ."

"How did you know that? She told me you stopped writing her or sending her any pictures of me while she was still in North Carolina, and that when she had tried to write you in Old Pine, you had moved and she couldn't find out where you went."

"I don't know about that. I know she worked in Chapel Hill, and I had a note from her sometime or other. We kind of kept in touch. I didn't see her, but we wrote. And then she came out here. I can't remember if she came out here by herself, or met this man and then came here, but I knew she was in California."

"Mama, now when she was pregnant, did you tell people you were?"

"Yes."

"You feigned pregnancy?"

"Yes. I just wore a big floppy something and then we'd stay gone as much as possible, she and I, antiquing or traveling. And I would be supposed to have gone down to Lake Magnuson to care for Mama, don't you know."

"How did Dad take all that, when it was happening?"

"Well, it was all right with him. But, Jimmy, it was me who did it. Oh, I have gone through hell with myself. And I thought a million times, oh my God, I am playing God. Roy told me that in the beginning. But I told him, oh, yes, it'll work out."

"What was the girl's name?"

"Rianna. Rianna Covington. There's a lot of them, and they're good country people."

"Why did you go to Stewart?"

"Well, that was good antique country, you see. And, like I said, she and I would travel a lot, and we didn't know exactly when it would happen and it just happened up there."

"Do you remember what hospital it was? Was it a private hospital?"

"No, it was just a hospital."

"What did you do about the birth certificate?"

"She used my name. Uh-huh, that was it."

"She signed your name to the birth certificate?"

"Uh-huh, yes. Or maybe I signed it. I've forgotten now."

"Well, can you remember back? Because it's important, Mama. I don't know when I was born."

"Well, Jimmy, you've got a birth certificate and that's right. The certificate is right."

"What date is it, then?"

"The twenty-sixth of June."

"But don't you remember that for years I thought it was July 12? And when I was talking with her, and told her about getting that birth certificate, she said that didn't make any sense . . . that I was born in April or May and that you must have signed your name to the birth certificate."

"Well, the doctor puts it on there, really. That's why she had my name when she went into the hospital."

"You didn't sign the birth certificate? She didn't?"

"No. Uh-uh. Your doctor fills that out."

"Then the birth certificate is correct?"

"Yes."

"Mama, when I was born—when I was born, was it a bad birth?"

"No, it was not terrible."

"Was she okay?"

"Yes."

"How long did it take to get back to Old Pine?"

"It was about a month, I guess, before we came back and then she went right on back to school, you see."

"What was her attitude? Then."

"Oh, she didn't seem to be too upset about it."

"I wouldn't think that she would be," I said. "I think she's a very strong person."

"Well, she has a number of children, Jimmy, don't you see."

"I beg your pardon?"

"I said . . ."

"No, wait a minute, Mama. Besides me, she just has one, a daughter."

"I thought she had several. And she married . . . now I can't remember if she told me that in a letter or what, but she had one, and I thought she had more than one. And I think the man she married was wealthy, wasn't he? Very wealthy? We kept in touch for a while, but . . ."

Her voice drifted off again, as though she was trying to remember something. I took her glass and made another round of drinks. I glanced back over to where she sat. I tried to feel something for her, but everything inside me was as cold as the ice I placed in the glasses. Only two things were in my mind—to keep her at ease and to ask, and get answers to, all the right questions. But some of the questions were coming out of nowhere, from a list I didn't know I had. I walked over, handed her the drink, and sat back down again.

"Mama, did you ever resent me? Like in the time I was coming up and I was so different from you?"

"Oh, no, I never . . . uh-uh. . . . Maybe you thought I did, but no."

"But there were so many differences between us. You never understood me. Neither did Dad. And I grew up always wondering why that was. Why was I so different? And I'll tell you, Mama. When that woman finally came along, when she told me, you want to know what my first thought was? I said to myself, well, that explains it. All these years . . . I knew something was wrong, something did not fit. And now I've finally found out why. . . .

"I mean, I knew you cared for me in your own way, but I knew also that it was harder for you to show feeling than to do anything else. And that was true of you with everybody. But it had a heavier effect on me because I didn't know whether you loved me or not." I tried to slow down, take the urgency out of it. "But now, I really don't have any hard feelings either way. I say that . . . no, I do have bad feelings, but those are things that . . . nothing could be done. . . . I mean, I don't know what kind of mother your mother was, but was she really hard in terms of

154

not showing her feelings? Because that's the only answer I can come up with if you loved me, even if another woman born me."

"Well, Jimmy, she didn't show feelings. She didn't."

I almost gasped as she said that. It explained so much. "And you were a direct product of that?" I said. "You never got any love?"

"That's right. My mother—I never remember . . . she never even kissed me. Not ever in her life that I know of."

"That's what I mean. It had to fit!"

"And I was forty years old before I ever appreciated her. And Jimmy, I must tell you that I thought, if there was ever anybody in this world I didn't want to be like, it was my mother. And I am just like her."

I looked at her pathetic little face. "Mama, did you ever regret doing it? About me being born? You've said you've felt guilty about it. But did you, have you ever really regretted doing it?"

"Oh, well, I was so glad to have you and all like that, Jimmy. I felt like you were a part of Roy. Roy was a fine person, and I loved him devotedly. We had awful times. But that's married life anyway. A lot of people do that. But I loved him devotedly. I just didn't handle him right. Our biggest difficulties were finances. He was one way, and I was another. And I should have talked out these things with him. But I didn't. I'd get mad, sulk up, and not talk them out."

"Mama, this thing about finances . . . that carried down to me. I mean, I don't remember ever having a birthday party . . . ever."

She nodded. "Uh-huh . . ."

"I never had one birthday party . . . and I never had Christmas, except clothes and shoes that usually didn't fit."

"I know that, Jimmy. And I was that way. And I regret to this day that I was born that way. Oh, I made every mistake in the book, I can tell you that. I really did." She stared into the fire, her jaw clenched. "You know, there are a lot of my friends who have told me things about themselves that I would never have bared to them. I don't have the capacity for opening up and telling. And it's bad, because I just keep everything inside. . . ." She shook her head grimly.

"Mama, maybe now you'll be able to. Maybe this will start you doing it."

"No, uh-uh. No. I'm a *very* private person."

"But that's the problem! I mean you've borne this thing for thirty-five years now. . . ."

"Yes. And don't think, oh, I weep to myself many times what people don't know about. Because I feel so bad about it. . . ."

"Why? Was it a mistake? Do you feel that?"

"Jimmy, I don't know. I just feel that I have taken things . . . well, there have been times when you have been upset and disturbed, and I have felt I have utterly failed you."

"But you failed me not because you intended to. You failed yourself. You see, Mama, the thing you have to understand is that it's where you came from. You were what you were. I am what I am. But, Mama, there's still hope for me and there's still hope for you. That's why I had to talk to you. You see, when I was young, because I never got any love, I now don't feel I can accept any love. But by talking about these things . . ."

She looked from the fire to me. "Well, honey, I'm glad that it's come up. That you know, and I know that you can understand some things. I know you must feel . . . and I can see where you would have felt that I just didn't love you or something like that . . . and you think, well, she's really not my mother and that's the reason that we've had these differences. But of course, that isn't it at all. I've loved you and do love you. But I don't show my love. It's hard for me."

"I understand you, Mama, I just wish you would try to understand me. There are some things . . . the fact you never gave me a birthday party or anything else like the other kids I knew had . . . things I was told in school I should expect from my mother."

"Yes. And I've realized that. But you see, I never had any of those things, so I didn't think they were important. But I know now."

We both stopped talking, verging on exhaustion.

"I have tried to rub it out—what happened—to have it in my

mind as though it never happened," she said. She seemed to be fading. "I don't know. . . ."

"Mama, that's natural," I said. "Now, there's something else I need to say. That cabin up on Sadler's Creek. I tried to explain to you that that place meant something to me, something important. Then I go there and the neighbors tell me you're about to sell it. The idea of selling that place! I mean, if you needed the money, why didn't you tell me?"

She bristled. "Now, Jimmy, I live on very little. I have some money invested that I get dividends on, but since things have gone up so much, I really did need the money."

"But, Mama, the important thing about the cabin, the reason that place is important to me is that . . . I've seen you sell out everything else from the family without ever considering me or telling me, but that place, I figured if there was anything that was my birthright, that place was it. I felt like, when is she ever going to give me one thing?"

Her dark eyes turned on me and her voice tightened in anger. "Jimmy. All right. You know what? You sent me a thousand dollars"—she was referring to a down payment I offered her on the cabin—"and you know where it is now? It's in your name and my name in the building-and-loan. See?"

Now I bristled. "But don't *you* see, that's still around the bend! What I'm saying is, I didn't want to have to ask you for the cabin. I didn't want to come up there one day and be told you were selling it out from under me. The thing is, I'm not trying to get something for nothing. If you needed money, I would have gladly given you money. But that cabin . . . I just would have rather done it in a way that wasn't a business deal."

The words came hard from her, with sharp, cornered syllables that hurt me with each inflection.

"I would, as Roy used to say, eat shit before I would ask anybody—you or anybody else—for money!"

I wanted to grab her by her throat and never stop squeezing. I wanted to scream her stupidity at her. Why wouldn't she, at this one important time, listen and hear and understand that I would have gladly paid her to give that place to me? To give it

157

to me! To, for one fucking time, say, here, Jimmy, this is yours. Why couldn't she hear what I was saying? But instead, I gripped myself and smiled at her.

"I respect that. . . . I respect what you say, Mama. But you are going to have to understand something now. If we're going to have . . . if we're ever going to have anything between us, there's got to be some compromises along the way. And you have never compromised in your life."

"No," she said, "I guess I'm stubborn as a mule."

"Okay, understanding that, that cabin up there on that creek . . ."

"Jimmy," she said, "every night, I pray for you. Just that you find yourself and reach your capacity and influence other people for good by your wonderful writings. . . ."

She kept on talking, subject dissolving into subject. I had to listen. I had to keep track and leave the other issue behind. I mixed another drink and listened. Then she brought up Ria. She had hoped, she said, that Ria would be all right.

"Ria's tough," I said. "But she doesn't have any real integrity. I mean, she sold out for money. She married for money. Now that's something my dad would never have done, I don't think. It's something you wouldn't have done. It's something I would never do.

"You know, Mama, you and I are never going to be close like a Walt Disney family, because we just ain't. There's nothing you can do about it, and nothing I can do about it. All we can do now is, now that we know everything there is to know, now we can appreciate each other for the way we are . . . and I think that's a blessing."

Words. Such worthless words. I was saying anything to keep the conversation going. Was I going crazy in front of my very own eyes?

"I think, Jimmy, oh, if I could only go back . . . so many things I would do differently. It's too late, of course, now."

"When you created me that way, which is what you did—"

"That's right. . . . I played God."

"But when you did, Mama, I can understand why you would

never tell me. You didn't see any reason to tell me. No one else knew but Dad, you, and her. . . ."

"Jimmy?"

"Yes, Mama?"

"I think I shall go to bed now. And you ought to try and get some rest, too. We're both tired, honey."

"Yes, Mama. We're both tired."

I had arranged with a neighbor to spend the night next door. I was too big to sleep on the couch and I didn't want to ask my mother to sleep there. Then, too, there was something inside of me that had known I would not want to spend the night in the same apartment with her. I needed privacy to review what we had talked about and to plan our next conversation.

I kissed her on the forehead, hugged her, and bade her good night. Then I left the apartment, walked down the stairs to the beach, and stood alone on the sand, smoking a cigarette and breathing the fresh air. I would have given anything for just one clear, clean, uncomplicated thought or feeling.

Next morning a fine rain was patting the sand into a dark, gray blanket. My sleep had been restless and I awoke stiff and sore. Walking back to my apartment, I tried to sort out what was left to ask, to say, to document. Everything the night before now seemed a jumble of sentences. I was supposed to be a trained questioner, but I had lost my way, sidetracked by emotion. *God, do we ever grow up and leave the child in us behind?* I shuddered, thinking of what a strong, compulsive force the child in me still was. If there had been a time when the child was meek and yielding, now he was tirelessly demanding. It was a dilemma. He was hampering my quest to document my origin. He was trying as desperately as I to have his say, to make his case. And he was winning out, causing me to stray from the agenda I'd established. I wished that he would go away. Didn't he know he was dead?

Edith was awake and dressed when I arrived. After a silent, nervous breakfast, we settled back into our seats of the night before. The tape recorder began running.

She started it off. "I'm glad, Jimmy . . . it'll take me . . . I mean,

159

I have to get accustomed to all this. You know, I have listened and read so much about adoption and children who weren't told and how some of them had reacted . . . and how shocked and everything they were. And I thought about that, because this would be an even greater shock to a person than adoption. And that's worried me, see."

"Mama, don't you think people should know who they are?"

"I guess so. But, Jimmy, you're highly sensitive. Now me, it would never have bothered me one way or the other."

"What *does* bother you?" I asked.

"Being alone and growing old, Jimmy. I do wish I had someone to live with me to help take care of that big house."

"I don't have many friends, Mama, but the friends I've got are really solid. The ones I got, they would do anything for me. They care about me."

"You were always wanted, Jimmy. In the worst way."

"I've always had the will to live, Mama. I've always had the will to survive, and I always did it on my own. I had help, but most of it came from me. It had to come from me."

"People are the way they are, Jimmy. Now I have always been a very determined person. If I could do something about something, I could make myself do it. In school, I aspired to be more than my station in life. I was determined that I was going to be among the top. And yet, Jimmy, when this other thing came up and I found that I was not going to be able to bear any children . . . that stumped me. I was just heartbroken. I never will forget it. I told Roy that I felt like I had failed him and that he deserved a child. Back then they were just beginning to talk about artificial insemination. So we talked about that and we talked about adopting. We talked about everything.

"I even went to Richmond, Virginia, about this artificial insemination. The problem was finding someone, some woman, who would go through that sort of thing. We talked back and forth, and the doctors in Richmond made efforts to find someone. But . . . we didn't want somebody who was a plain old nothing. I mean, after all, you've got to consider her register.

"So . . . we just couldn't seem to get anything done. And I even went so far as to talk to this girl, she had a child or two, and in talking around abouts with her, I tried to approach her about it. Well, she wanted us to adopt her children. I was not looking for something like that.

"Then there was another girl, but she was not the right quality. And I thought, well, maybe I could find somebody else. And then, in that interim, is when I got the other idea. To do it on our own, without the doctors. And it was me, Jimmy. I'm the one. I was looking for a good, sweet girl. And I found Ria. She came from a good family. We became friends. I liked her. And she was ambitious. I mean, she wanted more than she had. And so, it worked out."

"Mama, tell me the truth now. Did she know what she was going to be doing?"

"No. I don't think so. And yet . . . I don't know. That was one bridge I never crossed, and I didn't want to. I put it away. You don't know how much I have worried. When I think about it now, it makes me sick. I thought of a million things . . . what if you had been mongoloid or what if she had died . . . and I think, well, God punished me in a lot of ways, but he was good to me in that way . . . that nothing like that happened."

"Why do you think God was punishing you?"

"Well, I never understood in the first place why I couldn't have children. I thought, what have I done in my life? . . . Or maybe it was handed down to me. My grandfather was a rich man who created many scandals. He got two women pregnant, including my mother's governess, before my grandmother divorced him."

"How long did it take to convince Dad to do this, Mama?"

"Well, he was not too opposed to the idea. He was traveling, he covered ten counties, and before Ria, he went with some gal down near Johnston City. She was married to somebody else but they were separated. She had a son, and I think the son belonged to Roy. He asked for the child, and she said no. She worked in a shirt factory down there."

So. Somewhere I had a half brother.

"Then I took things into my own hands. I felt Ria was the kind of girl who needed something, and she was ambitious, and that we could help her and she could help us. We lived in the country then, in a little house outside of Old Pine. She stayed there with us, had her own bedroom. It just never came to the point that we ever got down to where Mama lived."

"How did you handle it when Dad was with her?"

"Well, I was doing quite a bit of club work then, so I was gone a lot and they had a lot of chances to be together. And we were all fond of each other."

"Did you pay her way through beauty school?"

"Yes. Oh, yes."

"How many years did it take to do that?"

"Oh, it didn't take but six or seven months. It was just a beautician school. But she was a good beauty operator."

"Mama, when did she get pregnant?"

"Jimmy, I can't remember. Maybe she didn't get pregnant until she was in beauty school. I can't remember. Then, when she was, we went to Virginia, stayed in Petersburg for a couple of months . . . had an apartment there, and then we went to Lexington."

"When she found out she was pregnant, did she tell Dad or you?"

"She told him."

"How did you handle the news?"

"I can't remember. . . . Oh, it was as though she had had an unfortunate experience or something like that. I don't know if she ever knew that I knew it was his child. I mean, we never discussed it. She was just pregnant, and we were happy to have the child."

"Did she want the child?"

"Well, I think that she would have, but, Jimmy, she was in no position to . . . I mean, she couldn't have kept . . . I mean it would have been impossible for her. And then, too, she knew we wanted a child terribly. We made that very apparent to her. We were just thrilled to death."

"You don't think she was in love with Dad, do you?"

"Well, I'm sure she felt a great deal for him. He was sweet and

162

nice and he had a lot of virility . . . a masculinity there that was very appealing."

"But you . . . you didn't feel bad about this when it happened, did you?"

"No."

"When did you start feeling bad about it?"

"When I started to realize what I had done. I was cowardly, Jimmy. I couldn't bear to think about it, or have anybody else know about it. I was always happy to have you, but maybe, I don't know, I just thought . . . well, I was upset with myself for deciding to do it."

"Did you ever think about it during my childhood?"

"Oh, yes. When I knew you were different. You know, you didn't give a darn about school. And of course Roy would have been happy if you had been mean and wanted to play football and that sort of thing. And I'd think, well, the Lord never meant for me to have children, and now I've done something, and maybe he's just not going to forgive me."

"What about my appearance, Mama? I do look an awful lot like her."

"Oh, indeed. But you looked so much like Roy when you were little. You were the spitting image of him as a baby. It was all right then, but I always had the fear it would come out."

"Did Dad ever think it was wrong?"

"I don't think so. I mean, he would not have done it if I hadn't wanted to, but he didn't ever regret doing it."

"Mama, I ask that because there were so many times when he and I were pretty much split. . . ."

"Well, no, he didn't regret it . . . because underneath he felt you would be okay. He'd say, 'He's going to be all right. He's going to turn out all right.' "

A silence fell then. Outside, the rain had intensified and, pushed by wind, pelted the window. The boom of the breakers came muffled from the beach below. I stood up and walked to the window and stood facing the sea. I turned to the little old woman sitting so alone in that big chair.

"Mama, do you feel better now . . . now that it's out?"

She looked up at me. "I will, Jimmy. But . . . it will take me a little time . . . to get accustomed to the idea."

"It's going to take me some time, too."

"I wish you had let me know when she told you, Jimmy."

"I didn't want to hurt you, Mama. I was afraid it would kill you. I felt like you had reasons for not saying anything, and I tried to respect those reasons. Until I couldn't."

"Well, Jimmy, I hope that it hasn't thrown you."

"It has affected me. But I had to find out from you. When Ria told me, at first I just . . . well, she kept telling the story over and over, and she wasn't consistent. I have . . . I had a lot of resentment toward her, because I didn't know the story and I caught her in so many different versions. She told me a couple of things that conflicted, didn't make sense, and I'm a reporter— I noticed all of them.

"But I don't think she really remembers what happened. I think when she saw my name she said, 'I'm guilty and I've got to make it up to him.' The thing was—is—Mama, she was a victim in a way. She was . . . and I was."

"Sure. Sure, Jimmy."

"So she doesn't owe me a goddamn thing, and this is something I have to tell her. The thing is, I really love her. People are human beings, and there's nothing wrong with being human. There's nothing *wrong* with what Ria did. There's nothing *wrong* with what my dad did. There's nothing *wrong* with what you did. And I'm not going to stand here for one minute and think that God would concern himself too much with this issue. I don't feel that my life would have been any different had I been born of you. Because you would still have been the same way you are. Just as Ria is the way she is. She's sensitive, but she has a gut-level survival instinct that is as tough as mine. I really think she saw a way out of her life back there . . . and she took it."

"I know it, Jimmy. She had no way of bettering herself, and she had to latch onto somebody."

"Well, I'm just disappointed in her because I know she is so dependent on other people. If she had just toughed it out!"

"She did the best that she could have done, Jimmy. Don't feel that way. She didn't have anywhere to turn. Her father was a gadabout, her stepmother hated her, and much of the time she stayed at her uncle's, his son kept trying to go to bed with her. She just didn't have anywhere to turn . . . there was nothing for the girl to look forward to."

Edith sat up in her chair and brushed her skirt smooth. "Jimmy, I think I am by nature a fairly good person. I have a lot of qualities that I sure don't like, but I have them. I think about my life and what I shouldn't have done. I hope that someday you will have a son. Because I'll be a better grandmother than I was a mother. You know that? That's the truth. I didn't *know* how sensitive you were. I never knew. I'm stupid. I admit that. I don't think I'm smart enough to analyze myself like you are able to. But I think we'll be closer now. Before I didn't understand you, and you didn't understand me. But no, I never treated you the way I did because you were somebody else's child. I just thought that was the way you were supposed to bring somebody up."

"Well, Mama, maybe we can. . . ."

"But I'm not sorry, Jimmy, about the way things happened, that you were born. And if I didn't love and care, I wouldn't have tried so hard to make you a certain way—even if I was wrong and it was the wrong way. Now I have learned that you have to let them have the flexibility that is inside them."

"Do you remember the time of the day I was born?"

"I believe it was early in the morning."

"Were you there?"

"Yes."

"Was Dad there?"

"No."

"How long before he saw me?"

"Well, just as soon as it happened, I telephoned him. I expect he saw you about two days later. He came up. And see, one reason for the mixed-up birthdays is that you were supposed to have been born in July."

"I was early?"

"Yes."

"How much did I weigh?"

"Oh, about nine pounds. You were a big baby. And then, well, I was into something then that was bigger than I was . . . and would have died if anything had gone wrong."

"Did anything go wrong?"

"No. No. I stayed right there."

"Did she have any problems with the birth?"

"Well, it took a right long time. I mean, nothing really serious, but her labor was a little bit longer than usual. I went in and I thought she looked tired and that sort of thing. It wasn't unusually difficult, but not the easiest either."

"How long was she in the hospital?"

"I can't remember that. But we had this practical nurse that stayed with her after that."

"She convalesced for a while?"

"Yes."

"Longer than usual?"

"No, not really."

"The doctor who delivered me . . . he's dead?"

"Yes."

"Did you ever want to tell me about it, Mama?"

"I don't believe so, Jimmy."

"Why?"

"I was too cowardly."

"What did you think I would do?"

"I don't know. I had read so much about the shock of such things and I didn't know what your reaction would be."

"Did Dad feel any guilt about this?"

"I don't believe so."

I let out a long sigh. "Well, now I feel I can go to Ria and explain this and she won't feel guilty about it."

"Well, she may hate me, Jimmy. But it wasn't exactly that she was chosen, but that it just fitted. It wasn't just a completely set up something, but yet it fitted and we could do something for her. One day, I might be able to see her. I couldn't do it now. I'm too wrought up. Now I worry about you."

"Don't. I feel relieved. I spent two years with this thing gnawing my guts. You've been a great help to me. Just a couple more things. Who did you tell the doctor you were? When Ria had the baby, I mean."

"I was supposed to be Mrs. Cook, her aunt. You know, I liked her a lot and so did Roy."

"Well, he had to love her a little."

"Sure. And I'm sure she did him. I mean, you were a baby. And it was sweat and blood and tears to get you here. You were wanted and wanted in a big way. I thank God for you. I ask forgiveness for myself, I don't ask him to forgive me for you, but for the sins I have done in my life. You know, when you told me you knew, I thought of that old saying."

"Which one was that, Mama?"

"Be sure your sins will find you out."

Another silence, this time a silence that said it was over. It was done. I clicked the tape recorder off. Edith sat staring at her hands. Outside, the rain had slackened. I took the tapes and placed them in their plastic cases.

The phone rang. It was Theresa. Edith had made plans to go out to the Valley and visit with her before her journey back to North Carolina. We said good-bye as though the past two days had not happened.

I walked back upstairs and poured myself a milk glass full of tequila. I crossed the living room, slid open the glass door, and stepped out on the patio, hardly feeling the raindrops hitting my face. Across the sea, Point Dume was barely visible. Down on the beach, a jogger and a big black retriever passed soundlessly by.

I lifted the glass to my mouth and drained it in one gulp. As the tequila went down, I found myself smiling vacantly and shaking my head. To think I had been afraid it would kill her. . . .

# Chapter 11

The hate came that evening, when Edith was far away in the San Fernando Valley and I was sitting alone at my worktable, staring at my reflection in the smoked glass of the picture window.

I hadn't felt it at first—just the heat of the tequila and the echo of the thousands of words that had been spoken in the past two days. The words were sometimes painfully hesitant, coated with remorse; sometimes staunch and unremittingly declarative; sometimes disturbly suggestive.

". . . now she had ambition and wanted to be something . . ."

". . . it meant something to her to have the influence . . ."

". . . she didn't seem to be too upset about it . . ."

". . . she wanted more than she had . . . so it worked out . . ."

It was then that the hate came.

Bitter air filled my stomach, as if it were being pumped in from some unseen source. The pains came in sharp, quick jabs and prolonged, rolling ripples that soon reached down into my intestines, squeezing and kneading and wringing them. The pain—the hate—spread upward into my chest. I began regurgitating air in short belches to keep my lungs from bursting. The belches lengthened until I was bent over, pushing the edge of the table with the heels of my hands, trying to expel what was exploding inside. Then came a high, piercing, pulsating ring in my ears. Higher, shriller, it intensified until there was no sound around me except that one. My eyes were closed tightly. Images began flashing in my mind—bright colored things that appeared, then disappeared.

I saw Ria as a young girl, lying in a deep green grass by a river bank, wearing a light cotton dress that was pulled up to her thighs. She was giggling at my father, who stood in front of her looking anxious and perplexed.

I saw her lift herself up to a sitting position and hunch her shoulders forward until her breasts pushed out over the top of her dress. She kept giggling, acting coy. Her dress rode higher over her thighs as she slowly spread her legs further apart.

I watched her reach up with one hand and touch the front of my father's pants with her fingertips, letting them move up and down over the fabric of his fly, gently pushing, then releasing. I saw my father's hand reach and touch her fingertips while his other hand began to unbuckle his belt. . . .

The ringing in my ears suddenly ceased. The pain disappeared. My eyes opened, and I realized I was on my bed. Outside, light stretched across the Pacific, giving definition once more to the horizon. Pelicans etched their slow way across the sky.

I swung my feet to the floor and stood up. My leg muscles were cramped, and I tried to flex away the stiffness. I walked into the bedroom, undressed, and took a long, hot shower. I changed into clean clothes, made coffee, and walked once again to the worktable. I sat sipping the coffee and waiting, watching the hands of the clock. I did not want to call Ria too early. It was still only 7:00 A.M.

I lit a cigarette and was about to get up and go check the driveway for the morning *Times* when I heard footsteps coming up my outside stairs. A key was inserted in my lock and the bolt turned. I tensed. Nobody except the owner of the building had a key to my door and he lived out of town. The door opened part way.

"Jim?" came a voice. "Jim? Are you awake?"

At the sound of the voice I relaxed. It was my neighbor, Eberhard Kronhausen, a psychologist who, along with his wife, Phyllis, also a psychologist, had been friends of mine for several months. In fact, aside from Theresa, they were the only friends I'd told about Ria and Edith.

"Come in, Eb," I said. "What brings you by so early?"

"Well, we were worried about you. We wanted to check to see if you were okay."

"Okay?"

"You don't remember?"

"Remember what, Eb?"

Eb nodded his head, smiling. "Ah, yes, of course you wouldn't remember." He walked over, patted my hand, and sat down in a chair beside me. "Well, my friend, for the last two days you have been, shall we say, out to lunch?"

I looked at him, not knowing what he was talking about. I shrugged, smiling, and said, "Eb, you know me, I'm always out to lunch."

Eb's face grew serious. "You flipped out. Phyllis and I have been very concerned about your safety."

"I don't understand, Eb. Edith came, we spent two days talking, she left yesterday and I was just getting ready to call Ria and arrange to meet with her and tell her what Edith said."

"Jim. Edith left here two days ago. You spent the night before last over at our place. We finally were able to get you back over here and to bed yesterday." He shook his head. "You were quite upset, dear boy. We didn't know how it was going to go for a while. You were drunk and really quite hostile. For four hours straight, until you finally passed out, you were raving about Ria."

I shook my head. Nothing. I remembered nothing. "What did I say?"

"What did you say?" Eb laughed. "My dear, what didn't you say! You called her a goddamn whore, a fucking slut! If you

170

could have gotten your hands on her, you would have killed her. Neither Phyllis nor I had any doubt of that. Oh, yes. You were very angry . . . very irrational. Pretty crazy."

I sat there, letting his words sink in. I looked around the apartment. My tape recorder was set up on the coffee table and the four "Edith" tapes were stacked beside it. My earphones were connected to the machine. I looked across the carpet at the fireplace and saw the shards of a tequila bottle scattered around the hearth. I looked back at Eb and shook my head again. "I don't remember, Eb," I said. "What in the hell happened to me?"

"Apparently you had just played back the tapes of you and Edith," he said. "And then you called us and said you were going to get Ria and force her to sit down and listen and admit to you the lies she had told you—"

"She?"

"Ria. You were absolutely convinced that everything Edith had said was true and everything Ria said was a lie. You started telling us Edith's version and, while Phyllis listened on the phone, I walked over here. That's the only thing that kept you from doing what you said you were going to do.

"Anyway, I got here and your door was open, so I just spoke your name and came in. You were too out of it to realize what was happening, and, luckily, you consented to come on over to our place before you went to Ria's. Then"—Eb shrugged—"it was just a matter of time before you finally wound down and we got you back here where you passed out. We came by and checked with you last night and you seemed okay. Maybe a little drunk, but at least calmed down. You didn't talk about going to Ria's, and we didn't bring it up. You also had a girl here with you, so everything seemed okay."

"A girl?"

"Ah, yes. Very pretty. Very nice. She was an actress, she said. She was fixing dinner for you."

"Why don't I remember any of this, Eb? I swear, I don't remember one thing you've said. I really was just about to call Ria and make a date with her, to tell her about Edith. But I

171

wasn't going to force her to listen to the tapes, or, for that matter, force her to do anything."

"Jim, dear, you apparently were under the control of your subconscious mind. I don't know. But you were drinking very heavily." Eb smiled. "I think you are okay now, though. So don't worry too much. And go ahead and talk to Ria. Just go easy on her. You are a very tough customer when you choose to be. So, just take it easy. Let time have its way. And we'll check back in with you later. Okay?"

I smiled and stood up. Eb hugged me good-bye and left. I walked over to the fireplace and began picking up the glass. I didn't question a word Eb had said. But what he had said puzzled me. He had been talking about a me I had never known.

Ria sounded glad to hear from me when I called. I had not told her Edith was coming to Los Angeles, and I did not tell her now. I simply said that I had something important to discuss with her, whenever she could break free from her schedule. I spoke the words calmly, indeed, almost lightly. I did not want to put her on guard. These days, she was already wary enough when it came to me. As it turned out, she was free that day. The new man in her life, a doctor from an old, very prominent Boston family, was attending a seminar in St. Louis. We arranged to meet that afternoon.

We changed cars at Ria's house, switching to one of her Rolls, and soon we were on the Pacific Coast Highway, heading north to Paradise Cove. I had made reservations at The Sand Castle, a beachfront restaurant near a fishing pier. We both ordered vodka on the rocks and after the second round came, Ria cocked her head and looked into my eyes. "All right, kid, let's have it," she said with a smile.

I lit a cigarette and let my eyes stray from her to the window. Outside a young woman was playing in the sand with two small children.

"Ria . . . I talked to Edith."

Ria's smile faltered, then disappeared. She straightened her body, almost, it seemed to me, as if she were steeling herself for

172

a punch to the solar plexus. She blinked several times, then quickly lifted her glass for a long drink.

"You called her and told her?" she said.

"No. She came here and I told her. We talked for two days. I got every word on tape."

"Is she still here?"

"Yes."

"Where?"

"Right now she's staying in the Valley with Theresa."

Ria shivered at that. Her arms suddenly were covered with goosebumps. Her eyes were darting nervously. I watched her, thinking I would give anything to know what was going through her mind right then.

"I need another drink," she said, waving to the waitress.

I ordered refills for both of us, and after they came Ria and I sat wordlessly for a while, she looking down at the table, me looking at her. Finally she looked up and smiled faintly at me.

"You really know how to surprise somebody, don't you?" she said.

I kept looking at her.

"Well, Jim," she said guardedly, her eyes narrowing, "what is it that you have to say to me?"

I didn't answer. Instead I kept my eyes on hers and sipped very slowly at my drink, keeping my expression blank.

"I . . . I . . ." She began to stammer. "I think . . ." She turned away from me and out to the open sea.

"Ria. Ria, she set you up."

Her eyes shifted in a flash back to mine and her face paled. "Wha-what?"

"You thought she never knew you were carrying her husband's child—but it was her idea in the first place. She admitted it. She was barren and desperate for a child. She found you, talked my dad into the scheme, and together they played you until they got what they wanted."

Ria's face froze as the words registered.

"I've got it all on tape . . . every word."

"Jim, let's get out of here, please."

I nodded, called for the check, and soon we were back in the Rolls, heading south. Ria sat silently, leaning her head against the window. Tears ran down her cheeks. She didn't attempt to wipe them away.

"Want to go to my place? Nobody would be bothering us."

I turned right at the Malibu Pharmacy and right again on Old Malibu Road. Soon we were at the apartment. She sat on the couch. "I would like to hear the tapes," she said.

"No," I said, shaking my head. "No. I don't think I could take that right now."

She got up and walked to the picture window and stood there with her hands on her hips. "Jim, make some coffee," she said, "I'd like a good strong cup right now." I made coffee while, across the room, she stood with her back to me. As I poured two mugs of coffee, she turned and came to the bar. Her face had regained its color now. In fact, it was almost flushed. She took the mug and sipped the coffee, still not really looking at me. When she finished the cup, she slammed it down on the bar.

"Goddamn her!" she shouted. "Goddamn her, goddamn her!"

I didn't respond, except to fill her mug with more coffee. She took it over to the sofa and sat down, cradling the mug in both her hands. "Do you know," she said, anger in every word, "I have spent the last thirty-five years of my life feeling ashamed because of that woman! Do you know that for thirty-five years I have felt so guilty . . . so goddamn, fucking guilty because I believed that she never knew her husband had raped me, had made me pregnant, and I was so sorry for her because she had been duped by him.

"All those years! Jesus, was I stupid! I felt so sorry for nice, dear, sweet Edith. I appreciated so much how she had been like a mother to me, had taken me away from my miserable life and had tried to teach me and show me so much of the big world.

"And when I found out I was pregnant, oh, how much did I appreciate her being so understanding and so caring. So caring. Oh, she was my friend! She wasn't going to let this poor little girl have to struggle with the stigma of having a child out of wedlock, no. . . . She would be so kind and wonderful and gracious and

174

caring and take the child to raise herself because she cared so much for me.

"Well, boy, she sure showed me the world, all right! And she sure did take care of me, all right!"

Ria turned to me and wrapped her arms around me, sobbing. She held me as tightly as she could, her body trembling from the crying.

"Oh, Jim, darling. How could I have been so naïve and stupid?"

She blinked away her tears and sniffed, moving away from me and regaining her composure. Her fists clenched as anger swept through her again. She tilted her head to one side and stared into space. Finally her hands unclenched, and she looked back at me. I had remained silently beside her.

"Do you know, Jim," she said, her voice shifting now from the plain, flat tone of hurt and anger to her lyrical Beverly Hills trill, "I always did suspect this."

"How could you have suspected it?"

"Well, I am psychic, you know. And that part of me has always hinted to me that I had been used. I—I guess I just did not want to believe it, actually."

She paused, as if waiting for me to say something. I heard the pause, but ignored it. I was thinking, remembering San Francisco and the beautiful time we had spent together. But the image of that kept shifting on its base, disturbed by too many other things that I was being forced to think about.

"Ria," I said. "There were some other things Edith said . . . things that . . . that don't quite go along with what you have told me. I . . ."

"Well, she's lying," Ria snapped. "I don't know what she told you but you can believe, baby, that after admitting what she admitted, she's going to try to make everything—"

"Ria," I interrupted. "Now wait a minute, Mama. Just wait a minute. Edith took full blame for what she did, and she really is sorry about it. She's sorry she hurt you, and she's sorry she hurt me. She really is. And I believe her. And you have to know that I understand there are going to be differences in her version

175

and your version. Too many years have passed. Memories don't hold all that well over all that time."

"Well, mine does," Ria said. "I haven't forgotten one thing about the horrible things that happened. You don't forget when you almost die, Jim. You don't forget when someone rapes you. And besides that, I do have a photographic memory."

"Okay. Okay. Just listen to me for a minute. There are a few things that I would just like to try and put together. Do you understand, honey? I am trying to piece together my life. And I'm not coming down on you. Hell, Edith's already exonerated you . . . if, in fact, that even needed doing. She's admitted screwing you over. But I still . . . and maybe it's just because I'm a journalist, but I still need to make one story out of the two that have been told me . . . one story that I can tuck away and say, 'Well, that's my story.' Do you understand that, honey?"

Ria leaned back against the couch.

"Okay," I said. "Now, again, I'm not doing a cross-examination, but I need for you to tell me again about certain things. When Edith was here she said first of all that . . . and don't get mad, now—I'm just telling you what she said. Anyway, she said that Dad didn't rape you, that you and he had an an affair that lasted about three months. Edith said she and Dad planned that, and that she would intentionally stay away from the house during the daytime when he was home, so the two of you could be together."

Ria said nothing. She stared down at the carpet.

"Another thing Edith said was that my birth was normal . . . that labor took a long time, but that you came out of it fine. Now, you told me that you almost died. . . ."

"I did almost die!" she blurted out. "I'm sorry. I didn't mean to interrupt you, Jim. Go ahead."

"Well, another thing she said was that she and Dad paid your way through beauty school. It wasn't much, she said, but she claimed they made sure you had everything you needed—to help you start your life anew. Now you told me that you put yourself through beauty school, and the only help you got was from Dad, who gave you his cigarette money without telling Edith. . . ."

Ria stood up abruptly and walked to the center of the room. She turned and looked down at me.

"Jim, what I told you—every word that I told you—was the truth. And is the truth. I'm sorry, but Edith is lying. She's lying because she's so guilt-ridden about what she did that she's trying to make herself look a little less horrible. But what she said is all lies, Jim. You must believe me. Why would I bring you into my life, why would I have risked destroying my own life in doing so, unless I loved you so much and knew that you needed to know the truth, no matter what the cost might be to me? I have no reason to lie. Edith has every reason to."

Ria walked over to where I sat and placed her hands in mine. "Would you take me home, now? I'm feeling very drained from all this. I had no idea . . ."

"I know," I said. "I've hit you with a lot. But you understand, Ria, I had to tell you."

"I understand. Now, Jim, please, take me home. We'll talk about this again . . . some other time."

I did as she asked. And everything seemed calm and all right. I was disappointed she didn't respond to my questions, but at the same time I understood how she must have felt—knowing for the first time that she had been used so totally by Edith.

When I got back home there was a message on the service that Edith had called. I returned the call and she said she was leaving in the morning.

"Jimmy, I can't talk to you right now, you understand, about what we talked about the other day. But, sweetheart, I promise you I will write you and let you know as much as I can remember about the matter. I love you, Jimmy. Just always remember that."

"I will, Mama," I said. "You have a safe trip home, now. I love you too."

I hung up the phone and just stood there, my mind too worn out to think about another single thought. Except one. I would have given anything if my father were still alive . . . if I could have had just one day with him. But that would never be. If I had been sad about that before, now I was angry. The more I thought about it, the angrier I became.

In the weeks following Edith's visit, being angry became my profession. Writing was almost an afterthought, both at the *Times* and at *True*. Since I was still writing for both publications, each blamed my increasingly poor performance on the fact that I was working for the other. To make matters worse, a few months before Edith's visit I had taken on the task of writing a motion picture treatment, something I'd never attempted before and had to learn about from scratch. It was all too much, and I was headed for some kind of professional disaster.

The anger by now had become another self, which came and went almost on its own. I could still control it at times—when I was with Ria, on the phone with Edith, or trying to write—but I was becoming increasingly manic and unpredictable. Whenever I was alone, sitting at home or drinking my dinner at a bar, the anger took me over without much effort. It was almost as if I welcomed it. It was as though I had finally found someone to trust. And when I really wanted to embrace it, as I now had come to do, I had found the perfect chemical combination to facilitate it: strong Colombian marijuana and the rawest of Mexican tequilas.

I did not tell Ria about these episodes. Our relations continued to be cordial. She seemed to be focusing most of her attention on Paul, the Boston doctor, who, she confided to me one day over the telephone, had proposed marriage. She sounded both skeptical and titillated at the prospect, and I was pleased for her.

But there was something else occupying my mind. I wanted Ria to sit down with me as Edith had done and tell me her story once more—this time with the tape recorder running. I expected she would say more or less the same things she had said before, but it had become very important to me that I have a record. I was sure I wanted this only as proof that, legalities to the contrary, I was indeed her son and she was indeed my mother.

One day I received a letter from Edith, postmarked Little Rock, Arkansas, where she had stayed with relatives on her way back to North Carolina. "Since leaving California," she wrote,

"I lived and breathed nothing but the past and our talk. Day and night I've gone over the past—all that I had tried for so long to blot out.

"(The years) 1937 to 40 I gave you briefly, but in going over all again I remembered more information and am trying to put it into sequence.

"I spoke to you of a 20-year-old girl that I got to stay with Mama just before or just after her operation. If she [the 20-year-old] had been suitable mentally and had had good inherent characteristics, the insemination problem would have been solved for us.

"Next came a blonde into the picture (I knew of her from living out in the country a few years before) that would have been okay but mentally not up to standard we wanted or required.

"Then came the approach through a friend with whom I had talked to her kid sister whose marriage had failed and who was in need of financial help. She had all the qualifications but she wanted us to adopt her two children. That was too much so that didn't work out, as we felt we certainly couldn't afford three children.

"Next came the girl Roy met (on the beach, I think) while fishing. As I recall, she was separated from her husband or there was some reason they were not together. She was much attracted to Roy and, of course, was most willing to sleep with him. He had told me about it in the very beginning. I was perfectly willing. A child resulted and he told her we would adopt the child and be very happy to do so. That she would not agree to, but wanted him to divorce me and marry her. So we were no further along.

"She was one who liked sex very much and Roy could not really be sure he was the father. He saw the child again about four years later and then he was sure, because of the great resemblance. The boy was about a year older (maybe a little more) than you.

"I had met two cousins whose father had a large family. He was maybe kind of a black sheep—think he, a farmer, sold whiskey (those were hard days, they lived way out in the country) to try to provide for his many children. The two older girls (either girl was okay) seemed mentally bright (very shy, as they'd never been anywhere), tall and certainly could have helped. I was a bit hesitant tho' about forming any ties or relationships there because of family relationships and someone in my family might become suspicious. So I was sorta uncertain—on the fence so to speak.

"Then I met Ria. Can't recall just how exactly but it was not at a dance or dance place, as I think I told you before. It was thru my antiquing, I'm sure, because while Roy fished I'd visit the whole countryside and visit with the people and I became acquainted with many people. Too, at that time, I always sought just the right person. Can't remember just how long it was, but I took her home with me.

"We both thought her a fine girl and liked her so much. Things had not seemed to go well for her and she could certainly have used some help. So we had, or shall I say, a close relationship grew between us all and then we sent her to beauty school. Can't recall dates and lengths of time now too much but because of so many difficulties that had gone before I had just about decided to give up and that adoption was the only answer. But then there was a quick conception and it was while Ria was at [beauty] school that it occurred. You've been told the happiness it brought and the wonderful gift you were and are.

"Because I am not perceptive, I think I never realized until too late that you were unusual and very sensitive as a child and I wanted and tried to mold you into the kind of person I am, that is, instill not my bad or, shall I say, weak characteristics but my best ones. In trying to do this I, by nature, as you so well know, an introvert and coming up in a time that to show any emotion was a great weakness, failed to meet your needs and now that you know the situation and since knowing it, you've questioned or feel I acted as I did because of it [the situation], I am crushed.

"No, no, I was trying to give you good principles, a good education and more advantages than Roy and I had as children. We both had had so much to strive for—we both wanted the best for you. Now I know the *best* as I considered it may not be the best. At the time I acted as I did, I thought it was for the best. I can see now why you rejected many things I considered important and now question many things I did. I just had a poor way of showing my love for you and meeting your needs.

"I'll try to remember from time to time and will certainly fill you in when we get together. Please, please don't discuss and discuss me with all your psychologists and friends. It makes me feel public and naked and inadequate. If you can be patient, other things may come back to me that you want to know. You and I will share and we will be *close* and I hope and am sure will have something now that the two of us can not only share but, in so doing, we will understand and have a bond of closeness that we never had before.

"Tho' I had a very odd way of showing it, I loved you always and love you now. I'm so proud of you and so are many others that you may not know too much about. Roy's folk would love you dearly if they knew you. . . ."

The letter was unsigned. I placed it back in its envelope and put it in a metal box—the same box that now contained the "Edith" tapes.

Now I was certain that I had to have Ria's version on tape. Someone was not telling the truth about the circumstances surrounding my birth. I reasoned that if I had Ria's version on tape, I could confront Edith with it and possibly gain more knowledge. Then I could tape *that* confrontation and make Ria listen to it. . . . and that, I was sure, would clarify matters even more— because I was sure I knew Ria well enough by now to know if she was lying. And by now, I suspected that she was lying, at least on certain details.

Edith was another matter. I believed that Edith was telling the truth, as far as she remembered it. She had admitted setting Ria up. She admitted failing as a mother. She had gone into great detail about each matter. She seemed truly contrite and remorseful, and it made no sense for her to lie, under those conditions, about details.

Throughout my life I had dreamed of a mother I could always depend on for warmth, for love, for security. If Ria was my real mother, I wanted her to be that ideal mother, and the conflicts between her story and Edith's were tearing me apart. If mine had been a normal birth, why did she insist it had almost killed her? If she had become intimate with my father over a long period of time, why did she insist he had raped her? If Edith and my father had paid her way to beauty school, why did she say they abandoned her? Why, indeed, unless she was guilty of something she could not admit. And if that were true, what was it? That there might be another, simpler reason did not occur to me.

At night, when I was alone, these things swirled in my mind, leading me more and more to the bottle and the grass that turned me into that other being that nurtured itself on hate. By day, reason returned. But as time stretched on, there was less and less of reason, less and less of compassion. Until finally there was a unity of day and night.

Now I was obsessed with getting Ria on tape so that I could stand in judgment and accuse her of being no better than Edith. Now I had come to hate both of them for what each, in her own way, had done to me.

Another letter from Edith arrived, written from another stop with relatives on her way home.

"Just came in. My folk here golfing in South Texas and that is good because I'm alone and can add a few more things . . . or, at least, be more certain with a few more pieces falling into place. I've lived with and thought of nothing else since we first began the discussion and tho' I'm still in a kind of state of shock, I am touched to the innermost part of my being and I have the most deep feeling and concern for you and an all encompassing love and compassion that evidently you never knew I had because I never showed it to you.

"I've always been aware of my inability to show my emotions, but never has anything like this hit me. Certainly I should have prepared myself for such a thing happening but I just refused to face such a possibility.

"You asked about when you were conceived and I told you it was during the time Ria was living with or visiting us when we lived outside Old Pine. After the visit there, she was at the beauty school in Raleigh, we keeping in touch of course, and Roy making trips there to the main office and seeing her.

"That was when it occurred, as I think back. It was not a quick thing and we had almost decided that adoption was the only thing to do. Then the miracle happened and we were so happy. When you came and I saw your little wrinkled face for the first time, my heart, poor as it may be, was filled with love for you—tho' you may think I've had a poor way of showing it over the years. Roy was so proud and happy and glad.

"So you may be assured that you were loved and wanted. Also I had that great feeling for Ria and there was nothing I wouldn't have done for her. My disassociation with her came only after I was sure she was doing extremely well and that her life was a complete one. I must confess that I wanted and hoped that there could be that disassociation. I have many good feelings but I'm also selfish and not the person I admire when I feel quilty and little.

"I will try to do all that I can because I want more than anything to get close with you and communicate. As I have said, you are all I have and I do love you and will do all I'm capable of to help you understand whatever bothers you. Another time I'm going to write about what you said about childhood unhappiness. I know that there were times of stress and strain and when I failed miserably. But I had no idea it was as deep as it evidently was.

"I remember some very enjoyable times . . . will take them up later when we write or see each other. As a very little fellow, you loved 'Little Black Sambo' and 'The Three Bears,' and I remember telling them over and over and your 'tell it again.' Our beach and crabbing trips—not all bad—but maybe me never making you feel warmth and understanding by me.

"My shortcomings were many, I know, but they were greater than I realized. My practicality was carried to extremes and I fight it even today when it is no longer what I consider a necessity.

"All of it is too much to cover and I don't want to go on and on. As I think over things and try to go back thirty-five years, I'll try to jot down what you will be concerned with.

"Do let me add, I hope you will make Ria understand that I feel gratitude, affection, and respect for her and sometime I want to see her. You were and are an object of love—never rejection on anyone's part. That you can always be sure of.

"Asking your waiting on me a little longer if you get impatient for quick answers . . . trying so hard to sort things out, I am your troubled but loving Mom."

As before, I placed the letter back in its envelope and put it in the metal box.

I then continued to ponder how I could get Ria to tell her story on tape without scaring her away. There were several problems confronting me on this matter. One was that Ria might construe such an attempt on my part as a devious effort to gathering enough information to sue myself into her trust fund. My dear sister certainly had planted that seed often enough for it to sprout. Another problem was Ria's new love interest. It was more than that now. They had officially announced their engagement and were living together. To make matters worse, Paul not only never let Ria out of his sight, but, on the few occasions I had been invited out with them, had shown a definite, however subtle, dislike for me.

The matter came to a head, however, before I had mapped any sort of good strategy. Ria called me one weekend night while she and Paul were in Palm Springs. Sounding very happy, and perhaps the slightest bit tipsy, she told me they had settled on a definite wedding date—the following month in La Jolla.

The conversation was brief. I accepted her invitation to the wedding, gave her my congratulations, and told her that I could only wish her total, complete happiness.

But after we said good-bye and my phone was back in the cradle, I let out a curse. I had not figured they would act so quickly. And once they were married, I knew I wouldn't have the slightest chance of getting her story on tape. I picked up the phone and dialed her Palm Springs number. She answered.

"Ria, there was something I wanted to ask you while we were talking, but your wedding news knocked it out of my mind."

"What is it, Jim?"

"Well, it's kind of private."

"Oh, well, that's all right. Go right ahead, dear. Paul had to make a trip downtown, and he'll be gone for a while."

"Well, I've been thinking about this for a long time and I need to ask you a very huge favor."

"Yes?" she said.

"I need you to tape-record your story about me."

There was a pause on the line. "No, I don't want to do that," she said, her voice becoming edgy.

"Are you not going to listen to my reason?" I asked.

"I don't care what your reason is, Jim. The answer is no."

"Look, Ria," I said, "Edith was willing to do it!"

"Jim, I don't care what Edith was willing to do. There's no way I am going to tape it. I told you the story as it happened, and that's the only story you're ever going to get. I don't know what you're trying to do, but it sounds a whole lot like you don't trust me. How dare you question my integrity!"

Her voice turned cold and even. "I think we've said all we need to say, don't you, Jim? It seems very apparent that you have swallowed Edith's lies and now, for some sick reason, you're trying to corner me. If you recall, I asked you if I could listen to the tapes of Edith and you refused. Now you want me to sit down and tape my side so you can compare the two and really show me and God knows who else what a liar you suppose me to be."

I hung the phone up very slowly and deliberately, so that the sound of the cutoff would say exactly what I wanted it to say: "As far as I'm concerned, Ria, you've just answered the question."

The next thing I remember, Eb and Phyllis Kronhausen were talking in the background. I opened my eyes and the room—their living room—came slowly into focus. I raised my head and looked out their window. The sun was setting behind Point

185

Dume. My head ached, my eyes throbbed, and the taste of tequila was still on my tongue. Eb looked over at me.

"Well, Jim, you did it again," he said gravely.

"The same thing?"

"Yes, well, almost the same. There was a variation this time. This time you said you were going to kill them."

"Them?"

"Ria . . . and Edith."

The Kronhausens served me tea and spent several hours talking with me, telling me about my latest episode.

"We feel we must warn you, Jim," said Phyllis. "This is quite serious business, potentially very dangerous. You've got to stop drinking right now. When the booze gets into your system you are losing all control."

Eb nodded. "Yes, dear boy. If you continue as you've been going, we can guarantee a tragedy. And quite possibly it will be your own."

"Besides your threats against Ria and Edith, you are exhibiting physiological symptoms that closely resemble those preceding a heart attack," Phyllis said.

I walked home that evening with their words in my mind. I did have one large drink. But only one. And when it failed to relax me enough to sleep, I took ten milligrams of Valium. I was not ready to die just yet.

The next morning I called Palm Springs. Ria answered.

"Ria, I'm sorry."

There was a silence at the other end. I was certain she was about to hang the phone up.

"Ria, listen, please. I was drinking the other night. I had just listened to Edith's tape again and I was upset. I didn't mean what I said. My emotions got the best of me. Please accept my apology!

"Ria, listen to me. I was out of my head. It won't happen again. I know you wouldn't have contacted me in the first place if you were living a lie. I know that you did it out of love. And I love you. It's just that I've been so mixed up lately. I haven't been able to see straight. About anything. But that's over now.

186

I realized that after I flew into you the other night. I realized I was wrong, Ria."

"We'll talk when I get back to Los Angeles," she said. "I have company here now, and I don't want to go into it."

"Sure, Ria. Sure. That's fine. I'll call you at home . . . when are you going home?"

"Monday."

"Okay, I'll call you Monday. I love you, Ria."

The call hadn't been as successful as I'd wished, but at least I had a toe in the door. Ria couldn't decide how sincere my apology was . . . and neither could I.

In the weeks that followed, I managed to moderate my drinking and my thinking to the extent that no wild mood shifts occurred. Ria remained cool toward me, but through my own behavior and a little inside work on the part of Ella, a workable truce resulted. Ella, who had worked for Ria eighteen years and had known about me for nearly that length of time, had always stood up for me and, even when I was acting crazy, let me know that she considered me as much a child of Ria's as Janet was. More important, Ella loved me and showed her love in ways that I needed far more than new suits and gold watches. And as important, Ria paid attention to Ella's counsel.

We began speaking to each other again, but the "talk" we were to have never took place.

Ria entered a rather strange, manic stage at this point, gushing to everyone about the new man in her life. The La Jolla wedding had become an "event" and despite Ria's assurances that it was going to be a small, modest affair, planning it occupied her every moment. Like every event in the social life she led, not one detail escaped examination and magnification. The *Time*'s social columnist devoted several paragraphs to the upcoming affair.

My role was to give the bride away. To that end, Ria assigned her dressmaker to tailor an appropriate suit for me.

The day of the wedding, our entourage departed Los Angeles early for the two-hour drive to La Jolla. Ria and Paul had arranged a suite for their wedding night at the oldest and most prestigious quarters in the area and, because of a last-minute problem with reservations, I was to stay in an adjoining room in their bungalow. The matter was hush-hush, said Ria, because Janet would be "furious" if she knew.

My own feelings regarding the wedding were certainly mixed. One part of me wanted very much for Ria to be secure with a good man who had the class, distinction, and money she required. But another part of me regarded all the great fuss over the wedding as somewhat overdone. And I had strong doubts about Ria's choice of a third husband. The good doctor seemed blessed with more than his share of pomposity. He also appeared to feel a general disregard and, indeed, arrogance, toward persons he considered beneath him. Of course, I didn't dare tell Ria my feelings. No one did. The empress had her new clothes and it was no one's place to say anything different.

The wedding was to be held at 2:00 P.M. The day was a La Jolla delight, with the fog nicely burned away and bright sunshine glinting off the arriving procession of Rolls-Royces, Bentleys, Mercedes, and even my own little red Porsche.

I knew the attendants from Ria's side, but Paul's friends were strangers, even to Ria. Beverly Hills is Beverly Hills and La Jolla is La Jolla and seldom do the twain meet. There was one woman in the La Jolla group, however, who caught and kept my eye. Surprisingly, she walked over to me.

"You're Jim Stingley and I am Delphine de Angelo," she said with a sly little grin. Her name was familiar. She was a professional dancer. "We have something in common, darling," she said, still wearing the sly grin. "I'm your new cousin."

Now her name was more than familiar. Paul had made a big point of bragging about his niece who had become a successful dancer.

I looked at her and immediately there was a strong sense of identification. She was tall, nicely built, and attractive in a striking, naturally sensual way. She had come to this main event dressed in brown cord slacks, an unchic tan blouse, and a brown jacket that had been worn rather often. Her blond hair was tossed and wild. Her blue eyes flashed at me.

"Isn't this just the most bullshit you've ever seen?" She said, her hand gesturing at the chic leading the chic.

I laughed out loud. "You noticed," I said.

"I noticed you," she said. "You and I are the only ones here who don't belong. Why did you come? I *had* to."

"I had to, too. But I'm glad I did, now. You can't know how much I've been wanting someone to walk up to me and say what you just said."

"What? About it being bullshit? My God, what else could any sane person think? Here's your mother dressed in white with a long white veil, my uncle wearing tails and a top hat, and they even had some fucking classic car brought here from Los Angeles on a truck so that they can drive away into never-never land—which, I must add, is three-tenths of a mile from here— like two teen-agers from the twenties. And this is the third marriage for both of them. I love it. It couldn't be any more insane. And yet look around us. Everybody here, except you and me, is taking this seriously. It's hilarious!"

God, had I found a friend. We talked until the church bell rang and the procession got under way. We were separated during the ceremony, but she and I kept glancing over at each other and sending private signals. After the wedding, we got back together again, this time sticking close to each other. The reception was held at the old hotel and, like the ceremony itself, was dramatically orchestrated, with elaborate giving of gifts and profound toasts. Delphine and I had smoked a joint on the way over and literally were pinching each other blue to keep from laughing out loud at what was supposed to be a most serious expression of faith and enduring love.

After the reception, we drove to a beach where we walked for hours, talking about our careers, our mutual contempt for the lifestyle of the newlyweds, our attraction to each other.

"You must be careful, Jim," Delphine said, her big toe drawing a circle in the sand. "I was raised among all of this and know enough about its fakery to survive. You're pretty naïve, darling. In this world, that could be fatal."

We left the beach when the sun disappeared into the Pacific

and made our way back to my room. We entered the bridal suite through a side door and immediately heard Ria and Paul engaged in a fierce argument. A door separated my bedroom from the living room and we couldn't make out what the fight was about. Finally it sudsided and there was quiet. Delphine stretched out on the bed. Moments later, while I was still standing by the door, we heard the front door of the bungalow shut and their car start.

"Whatever it was, they're over it," she said. "And now though deep inside they probably are hating each other, they are going to a special wedding dinner—which, I might add, we were uninvited to attend—and they will present themselves in all their radiant luster." She said this while rolling another joint. "Meanwhile, darling cousin, we are here."

She did not have to say any more. We made love. We smoked. We made love again. It was bizarre. It was beautiful.

The next morning we awoke to the sound of what apparently was the wedding breakfast. We lay beside each other and giggled like two ten-year-olds. Finally, Delphine bit her lips and assumed a facade of calm. "You are going to have to get dressed, James dear, and go in there."

I looked at her. "The hell I am. *You* are the one who's got to do it."

She folded her arms across her breasts. "Sorry. You brought me here. You're responsible." She snickered. "Besides, this is *your* room."

We went back and forth until finally I knew she wasn't going to budge and that I was going to have to make an appearance. I dressed quickly and, after combing my beard and moustache, I very firmly scrunched my denim cap on my head and opened the door.

Ria and Paul were seated at a glass table. Eggs Benedict, sweet rolls, a fruit bowl, juice, and coffee were being served by an elderly room service waiter.

"Well, good morning, Jim!" Ria said brightly, her face flushed and smiling.

"Yes, James," said Paul, "come join us."

I smiled back at both of them and sat down. "Well," I said, "and how are the newlyweds?"

Ria reached across and placed her hand in Paul's. "Marvelous!" she beamed. "Absolutely marvelous! And how was your night?"

Just then the door to my bedroom opened and Delphine entered the room, looking exactly like someone who had just climbed out of bed after an all-night orgy.

"Well, good morning, darling," said Paul to his niece, his smile still firmly affixed to his face. "Surprised to find you here." He chuckled edgily, looking over at Ria.

Ria never noticed Paul's smile. She was looking at me. Pure loathing was pouring from her eyes.

# Chapter 12

After La Jolla Ria refused to speak to me. This time there seemed no repairing the damage. She refused to discuss what had happened and, for the first time, I made no attempt to mollify her or apologize. I simply no longer wanted to be near her.

If I believed anything now, it was that I had been a pawn between two women, each seeking her own satisfaction, each finally seeing me only as a disturbing reminder of something neither could wash her hands of. So it was done. As I had always been, I was again. Except for one significant difference. Now that I knew, a coldness settled inside me, killing any taste I had had for optimism, for hope, for tenderness. If there was a gentle thing left within me, I did not want to feel it.

I constructed a new life to match my new attitude. I divorced myself from acquaintances, except my friends the Kronhausens. I changed my unlisted telephone number. I traded in my Porsche for a yellow Volkswagen "Thing," the ugliest, oddest vehicle I could find. I removed Ria's golden watch from my wrist and tossed it in the metal box that contained Edith's letters. I almost always worked out of my apartment, conducting interviews there, writing the stories there, appearing at the *Times* and *True* only to deliver the stories and discuss the next assignments. With rare exceptions, the pieces I wrote were less and less journalistic and more and more a reflection of however I happened to feel on a given day. The new Stingley evoked disappointment in those professional peers who cared and contempt in those who did not. I honestly did not give a damn.

In my private life, I added to my list of female acquaintances who excelled in bed. If one asked for more, I ended the relationship. Since most of them were as frustrated in their own way as I was in mine, this problem seldom arose. Those lovers who had been friends of mine, with whom I had shared my feelings and thoughts, now drifted away. What I wanted now was not companionship but a physical contest that I could always win.

When I was not with women, I was at a bar. The Crazy Horse Saloon and Alice's were my haunts. But the new me no longer enjoyed sitting alone and watching people. Now I went to fight. Because of my size, and possibly because other men sensed the dark energy that flowed from every pore of me, the fights were rare. I simply became a man nobody got in the way of. When they did, I shoved. And waited gleefully for them to shove back.

Spring came and the Malibu headlands began turning gold as the wild mustard bloomed. It was a season I had always looked forward to, but this year of 1975 I was blind to it. By now I was tiring of everything, even beautiful women. All they were to me were bodies. I was growing weary, too, of the chip on my shoulder, of provoking incidents even when I had no heart for them. I began to stay at home more, sitting at my worktable, writing letters to the person I used to be.

"He woke up one March morning and discovered himself absent.

"The cat was there, curled like tan smoke around the hearthplace. The Boston fern was there, hanging green but thirsty. The creeping Charlie was there, slowly tickling the philodendron. The typewriter was there, like a gray, Royal rock.

"But he was not there.

"A search of the bathroom turned up two *Playboys* and a box of kitty litter, one roll of yellow double-ply toilet paper, and a rusty pair of scissors.

"A search of the bedroom turned up the king-size bed ... empty, wrinkled, not entirely void of Colonel Sanders's extra crispy crumbs. And there were the closets full of clothes he never would wear because they were a him he never felt safe with ... and the shiny patent leather shoes that didn't fit either.

"The jar of marijuana was there, too. And the pipes. And the pictures of the mother whom he could not yet forgive.

"They were all there. Objects of matter. But no matter. Because he was nowhere to be found.

"And in the alcove that perches above the waves, the black table stood covered with notes to nobody. And the box beneath the table, filled with words from whoever he was when he wrote them. But he was not there.

"There was a note on the door. 'I am gone,' it said, 'in search of me.'

"The cat stretched, uncurling its smoke. The plants quivered with the force of an incoming wind that managed to blow through the sliding glass doors.

"In the corner of the living room, almost hidden, sat a bear ... shaking his head. It was not the best bear head one had ever seen, but it was an earnest head and it shook with purity. 'There must be a him somewhere,' he said, concern furrowing his face. 'If only he can find him.' "

Another day. Another letter.

"My friends the Kronhausens say I've been using my mother as an excuse for not tending to business. The business is simple ... whether to take a big swing at success, or stay safe, or quit.

"For many months now, I've successfully avoided dealing with the reality of the situation. I have done everything in my power to undermine the confidence of my employers. In the case of *True* magazine, it seems to have worked ... though that hasn't been finalized yet.

"Taking the shot. Laying everything you are on the line. That's been the bugger. The impulse to run is great. To quit. To die. To do anything but take the shot. No reliable security. It means giving up the job with the *Times*.

"The *Times* has been my security for five years. Not me. Not my own belief in myself. The *Times* has built-in respectability . . . people are impressed. Without the *Times* I am just another human. Even to my mother."

March came and went. The days and nights had the sameness of a sad song sung too many times. Every night now I sat at the Crazy Horse bar, drinking my keep-me-sober coffee-tequila combination and waiting for my body to tell me it was time to go home and to bed. Now I rarely noticed anyone around me. Bodies would sit next to me and then be replaced by other bodies, voices would drift around me and then be replaced by other voices, and I rarely noticed either.

Only when I first entered the bar, usually around 6:00 P.M., would I talk with anyone. Most of the time it would be Greg, the bartender, a laid-back Californian who, like most good bartenders, had a repertoire of entertaining stories to tell when business was slow and an ear was wanting to listen. One Monday, April 7, 1975, Greg and I were discussing cats. I liked mine, he hated his. I was sitting on the bar stool next to the waitress station. A cocktail waitress reported in. She was the new early-on girl. I smiled at her and continued talking to Greg about my cat.

"I used to have a cat," the girl's voice said, "back on my farm."

"Where's your farm?" I asked, as Greg walked away to wait on his second customer of the day.

"In North Carolina," she said, smiling.

"Where in North Carolina?" I asked, not believing what I was hearing.

"Outside of Chapel Hill," she answered. "I really loved it there. The cat's name was Steven Orlac. He was a love pig. You could start scratching him on the head and raise your hand and he would keep on raising up for more until he was on his tiptoe."

As she talked I began to notice her . . . and to notice that I was noticing her. Whoever this lady was, she had an aura that encircled her entire body, starting from deep within her gold-flecked brown eyes and spreading the length and breadth of her.

Just as seductive were the words she was saying. They stirred old feelings, made me remember what I had had back in the mountains of North Carolina, made me wonder—if I lifted her from where she was standing and placed her in the middle of them—how she would look standing there . . . with me. The image formed and was good.

I never moved from that stool the entire evening. When she wasn't waiting on a table or placing an order, her eyes never left me, nor did mine leave her. At some point she did mention she was married. But there was no significance in that statement. She might as well have been placing another cocktail order.

When I went home that night I did not think of Ria or Edith. I did not write myself letters dwelling on how empty my life was. All I could think of was her. I couldn't even remember her name. I hadn't noticed what her body was like. All I knew was that I might as well have been hit by lightning. All I knew was that for the first time in my life I had met this woman that was me. I stood out on my patio in the night sea air. I was so confused by my emotions that I did not know what to feel.

In the nights that followed, I could not keep myself from that bar stool. We talked about as many things as we could squeeze in. At one point, when Greg was out of range, I said to her, "You know, if you weren't married, I'd be on you like a duck on a June bug." I didn't smile when I said it. She looked straight into my eyes and blushed.

Each day the intensity increased. Finally, one evening I asked her if she would come to my place for a drink after work. I waited until she checked out, and then she followed me the two miles to my apartment. Inside I poured her a glass of wine and proceeded to nervously tell her everything that I could think of to tell her about me. I read her poetry. I showed her my Pulitzer nominations. I told her how I'd found out, just three years before, about Ria and how the whole thing had flung my life into a sometimes frenzied, sometimes candy-coated craziness.

We never touched the entire time. It was as though if we did,

196

we would not stop. It was as though we were scared to death that we would touch. When she left, I walked her to her car and stood with my skin burning as she slowly drove away, toward her home and her husband.

By now I knew her name. By now it echoed in my mind as I said it silently over and over, as if saying it would make her return. Loralee.

The next night she came to my apartment after work again. It wasn't that hard for her; her husband was always asleep when she got off work and forbade her ever to wake him. This time when I handed her the glass of wine, I pulled her to me. We just stood there looking into one another's eyes, not saying a word. This time we were not afraid to touch.

The next night the same thing happened. Neither of us could stop it, neither of us wanted to stop it. But after we made love, we talked about her being married, and I told her something I had never told another woman in my life. "I want you," I said, "to have my baby." After I said those words, we held each other tight for a long, painfully beautiful time.

Her fourth visit came several days later. She had lied to her husband, saying she had to come into work early. But I kept her too long, and when she didn't turn up on time, the manager called her home. Her husband answered the phone.

I was across the street from the Crazy Horse Saloon at Alice's after she went to work. The bartender nodded to me, saying there was a call for me on the house line.

"The shit's hit the fan," she said.

"What?"

"He knows. The manager called him, looking for me, asking why I was late. He's coming over here now. Please, Jim. Don't come here tonight. He's mad as hell. I just talked to him and he got it out of me that I was with you. I've got to hang up. I'll see you tomorrow."

I gave the phone back to the bartender, drained my glass of tequila, and started toward the Crazy Horse. Something inside me said there was no way he was going to hurt her . . . or have her.

Loralee almost dropped her tray when she saw me enter, I searched the crowded room for her husband, whom I had met one night at the bar. I spotted him, standing by her station. He was slender, tall, good-looking. But this night his face was pale and he did not look good at all. I walked over to him and I could see Loralee cringe.

"You can't have her," he said. "She belongs to me."

I looked up at him—he was two inches taller than I—and smiled. "She belongs to herself, son."

I was ready for whatever came next. But nothing came. He just stood there glaring at me. Still smiling, I backed away and sat down at the bar. I was there to stay—until something happened. Meanwhile, a distraught Loralee went about her work, carrying trays of drinks back and forth through the space, about six feet, that separated her husband from me.

I kept hoping he would make a move that would give me cause to take him outside and dismantle him. The man had no idea what kind of a crazed situation he was dealing with.

The crowd began to thin as closing time neared, and Loralee managed to come over to where I sat. She was very upset, close to hysterics.

"Look," I said, "nothing's going to happen. I'm not going to fight him. This is too serious for that. I'll leave and you go on home with him tonight and talk this thing out. Let him get it through his head that it's over, that you're not his property anymore. And I want you to be sure, yourself, too. Okay? You have to be sure yourself. I don't want to step into something and mess it up if you are going to have any doubts about it. Okay?"

She looked at me and nodded. Her husband was watching and I wanted so very much to hold her and comfort her. But at this point I didn't dare touch her. "I'll call you in the morning," she said, managing a smile. Then she turned and went back to her station to pick up an order that was waiting.

I paid my tab and eased off the stool, looking over at her husband. I nodded to him and I left, pushing through a small crowd of dancing couples until I reached the door that led outside. Standing on the sidewalk, I realized my hands were shaking. The whole thing was out of my control now, and all I could do was wait. I had never felt so helpless.

I tried to sleep that night, but that was impossible. I tried to write my feelings down, but my fingers only fumbled at the typewriter keys. Finally, I made a large pot of coffee and sat up in bed, watching the all-night movies on television. But I wasn't seeing what I was watching. All I was seeing was the image of my woman, her gold-tinted brown hair falling gracefully to her tanned shoulders, her gold-flecked brown eyes.

Exhausted, I fell asleep for several hours. At 9:00 A.M. I woke up and sat down beside my telephone and began to wait.

Two hours and many cups of coffee later, not one ring had sounded on the phone. Suddenly there was a knock on my door and I almost fell down hurrying to open it. As the door swung back, my heart sank. It wasn't her. It was Jimi and Dave, married friends of mine whom I had invited for lunch that day.

I asked them in, served coffee, and tried to explain what was happening. By the time I had finished my tale, both of them were astonished. I was the last person they'd expected to encounter in a state of desperate love. Dave, a leader of the Los Angeles Police Department's number one SWAT team, was looking at me as if I had slipped my tracks. Jimi, his wife, just stared at me with affection and amazement. Years later she would tell me, "I'd never seen a man express feelings like that."

Another hour passed. I kept apologizing to them for having to hang by the phone, while at the same time I kept telling them how much I loved Loralee and how I felt that my life hinged on what she would say when she called. They sat with me, waiting it out.

I kept making and drinking more and more coffee, carrying the phone with me every time I moved anywhere in the apartment. When I sat down, I kept the phone in my lap. When I made coffee, I set it down on the counter beside the stove.

When the clock showed 12:45 P.M., my heart began to sink. "She's not going to call," I said. "Maybe he's convinced her that this is just some crazy thing. Maybe . . ."

The next maybe was interrupted by the ringing of the telephone. The atmosphere was so intense that Jimi, Dave, and I jerked at the sound. I let it ring a second time and then picked up the receiver.

"Stingley," I said.

"Jim?"

"Are you all right, girl?"

"I'm okay. We talked all night. I finally told him I can't live with him any longer. We've agreed to split."

"Are you coming here to me?"

"Do you really want me, Jim?"

"I really want you."

"Can I bring Toby, my dog?"

"You can bring Toby, you can bring Dumbo the Elephant."

She let out a long breath. "Okay," she said, her voice sounding so fragile, so far away. "I'm coming. I've got to pack a few things, but I'll try to be there in an hour. Oh, Jim, I love you so much, baby. I love you so much."

I started crying. My heart seemed about to burst. "I love you too, Loralee. You come on home now. You come on home to me."

"I'm on my way," she said. "I'm on my way."

## Chapter 13

After Loralee came, I lived in the same apartment, worked at the same jobs, had the same friends, ate in the same restaurants. Yet every morning I felt I was setting foot on unknown ground, a new world in which "happily ever after" was not just the concluding words of a fairy tale. Loralee had brought me back to life, and we talked endlessly about the new life we would have. Our dream was to return to the land I was buying from my mother in North Carolina. The only house on the property was a hundred-year-old cabin, which we would renovate and surround with gardens, greenhouses, vineyards, and orchards. Down by the creek I would build myself a studio where I'd write my first novel. And we'd raise our kids there, far from L.A. smog and hypocrisy.

During the day I went to work much more happily, while Loralee, freed from the waitressing job she'd hated, sunbathed in the nude, giving her body a golden glow and giving herself some slow time to unwind from the tensions of a marriage that had failed. To me, life seemed perfect. Ria and Edith were distant memories, bad dreams forgotten. I spoke of them to Loralee with such bitterness and finality that she assumed they no longer played any part at all in my life.

Eventually, of course, reality paid us a return visit. The first form it took was a telephone call from Loralee's parents, upset by the rapid dissolution of her marriage and the speed with which she and I had set up housekeeping. Even long distance from Tempe, Arizona, her father sounded capable of spitting nails as he ordered her to appear before him and tell the whole story. We talked it over, quickly agreeing that such a visit would be in order, and she departed for Arizona while I stayed in Malibu and sweated out the hearing.

Two days later she returned intact, but with the information that her father was coming to Los Angeles on business and wished to meet me. I prepared my defense and, accompanied by Loralee, met with him in a two-hour session in which I argued the honorableness of my intentions. He left the next day at least partially satisfied that his daughter and I were very serious about each other and fully intended to consummate those feelings in marriage as soon as legally possible.

My honeymoon period with Loralee, already assaulted by her father's skepticism, ended abruptly after his departure. I returned home one day to find Loralee in a temper about the various nude photographs of old girl friends that adorned the walls of my bedroom. And that was not all. She had tried to look upon the photos as art, she said crossly, but there was nothing artistic about the women's undergarments, in varying sizes, that she kept finding tucked here or tucked there. I took all this ire as a minor side effect of her father's visit, until I returned home one afternoon to find all of these items disposed of. It was our first fight. I argued that she had no right to tamper with my belongings. She argued that she had chosen to live with me, not my past.

"That's silly," I said.

"Don't tell me it's silly," she replied. "While you're at work, I answer the phone all day and listen to about a dozen different women ask who I am and when you're going to call them."

"Oh," I said.

In the days that followed I made it known to my past female bed acquaintances that I was no longer available in any way, shape, or form, and we soon settled into the close-knit, romantic routine of two people who had spent their lives looking for each other.

Something else occurred at this point. For the first time in a long time, I wanted to see Ria. I wanted her to meet Loralee. I told myself I was not seeking Ria's approval but that I simply wanted her to see this person who had turned my life around. I asked Loralee if she would like to meet Ria, if only to see first-hand the unreal world of the very rich. She admitted she was curious.

But when I called Ria, she was less than receptive. I had forgotten the rift that existed between us. Still, she did not hang up on me and I was able to tell her about my new life. The enthusiasm in my voice seemed to register with her. I could tell that at least her curiosity was piqued.

In the meantime, I'd been having a recurring thought about Loralee. My eye told me that she had the natural makings of a model, particularly, I thought, in the commercial field that called for those tall, sexy but clean-cut, All-American girls. I had a friend in Los Angeles who was a prominent professional photographer and, through him, a portfolio was shot. My hunch was right. Within a week, she had her first assignment.

I called Ria again to see if we could get together, not failing to tell her of Loralee's new career. This time she agreed. She said she and Paul would be attending an antique gun show at the Ambassador Hotel that Sunday and invited us to join them there. She said she and Paul would be decked out in period costumes, as would be the other participants in the charity event.

Loralee, who had a wardrobe of period clothes from her grandmother's attic, dressed in costume for the occasion, and I took along my Nikon and an assortment of lenses.

The meeting went well, Ria and Loralee liked each other instantly. I wasn't sure how to act, so, after introducing them, I spent my time taking pictures of them around the various vintage weapons. Ria put her arm around Loralee for some of the photos and soon the two of them were talking to each other about modeling, North Carolina, and, I suspected, me. Driving back to Malibu that afternoon, I asked Loralee what she thought of my other mother.

"I liked her," she said. "She's a lot of fun. She seems like a very warm, very nice lady."

I nodded, not saying anything.

"I wish you didn't have such a problem with her, Jim."

"I wish I didn't, either, Loralee. But I do. There's a part of her I want to love so much. But there's a part of her I hate."

Loralee looked at me. I had told her before of the hate and she hadn't said anything. Now she was looking at me in a way that was just slightly strange.

"That hate . . . it scares me, Jim. It just doesn't seem to be something that should be part of you. I don't understand the hate."

"There's no way," I said, looking at her coldly, "that you could understand." We were silent the rest of the way home. I had suddenly plunged into that black place that I had thought Loralee would keep me from ever plunging into again.

Back at the apartment, she changed clothes and, without saying anything, left with her dog for a walk on the beach. I sat at my desk and watched her walking south, her head down, her hands in her pockets. I lit a cigarette and looked out at the afternoon horizon. Slowly my body eased, until, thirty minutes later when she returned, I was relaxed again.

"I'm sorry," I said to her. "Sometimes I can't control those feelings."

"It's okay." She smiled and walked over to hug me. "Maybe I can help you with that, some day."

I hugged her back. "That . . . well, we'll see. Let's not talk about it anymore right now, okay? Let's go to Alice's and have dinner."

She nodded, her smile more subdued than before.

Dear God, I thought to myself, please don't let her get in the middle of this!

Ria called me at work the next morning.

"Jim, can you talk?"

"Sure, Ria. I was just transcribing some tapes."

"Well. I just wanted to tell you what an absolutely delightful girl that Loralee is. And I also wanted to tell you that yesterday was the most comfortable I've felt around you in a very long time. I don't know what she's done, but whatever it is, she's a very good girl for you. Top-notch! And I would like to get to know her better. Why don't the two of you join me for lunch Saturday at The Bistro?"

I paused, not knowing quite what to say. I had not figured on such an aggressively positive reaction from Ria, and somehow I didn't trust it.

"Jim? Are you still there?"

"Oh, I'm sorry, Ria. I was just trying to remember if we're free Saturday."

"Well, darling, why don't you find out and call me back. And, oh, does Loralee have the right clothes for The Bistro? Because if she doesn't, she can slip into something of mine. We're about the same size, aren't we?"

"Well," I laughed, "I think you've got her in the chest department; otherwise you're about the same. But she's got clothes. I'll check with her to see if we're free and get back to you. And, by the way, you're right about her, Ria. She is good for me."

"Well, good, darling. Just make sure you treat her better than you've treated the others."

When I hung the phone up, I leaned back in my chair, thinking about her response. I still didn't trust it. And I felt myself resenting her last remark.

That evening I told Loralee of the invitation. Her eyes lit up at the mention of The Bistro. I left a call with Ria's answering service that we would be there.

The lunch went extremely well for the two of them. Ria marveled at Loralee's story of how she and I had come together, then it was Loralee's turn to marvel as Ria told "our" story for what now had to be the quarter-of-a-millionth time. In this version the rape took place in a swamp, with Ria flung to the ground on a coat that Edith had loaned her.

I sipped vodka after vodka, trying to appear calm as well as interested. But I kept hearing Edith's version ringing in my ears and I kept wishing I had never told Loralee anything about the story, much less introduced her to Ria.

When we got home that afternoon, Loralee made coffee and the two of us sat on the patio. I maintained the silence I had fallen into at lunch.

"She loves you, Jim," she finally said.

I kept staring at the sea.

"She really does, Jim. She really cares about you. She's so proud of what you've accomplished. She feels so guilty about what happened, but there wasn't anything she could do about it then. Now, well—while you were away from the table those two times, she told me she knows you haven't begun to reach your stride in writing and she's willing to do anything she can to help you. She thinks you will be very good someday."

"You two have formed a really sweet little club, haven't you?" I said sarcastically, still looking out at the sea. "Well, next time the club meets tell her I don't need her goddamn help. When I did need it, she was too busy helping herself!" With that, I smashed my coffee mug on the deck, and Loralee froze in fear. I stood up. "I thought," I said to her, biting off each word, "that you were different. That you were special. I should have fucking known better. You're like all the rest of them!"

Trembling now with rage, I left her sitting there and walked down the stairwell to the garage. I got into my car and roared away, not knowing or caring where I was going. I drove north to Oxnard as fast as the car would go. Finally the rage started to subside and I turned around and headed home to apologize. When I got there, she was gone. So was Toby, her dog. She had left a letter on the bar.

"Dear Jim," it began, "I want so much to love you, to be with you for the rest of my life. But there is an anger in you that scares me. There is a hatred inside you that, when you turn it on me, leaves me literally in fear of my life. And I cannot stand up to that. It is too strong and hurts me too much. I have already been hurt too much.

"Toby and I have packed up our things and gone to stay with a friend. This is the only thing I could do. I can't stay here with you as long as you can, in the flash of a moment, turn that terrible hatred you have on me.

"I am crying as I write this. I want to be with you—the real you—so much. I need the real you so much. But you are allowing yourself to be . . . I don't know what . . . but not a whole person. And I have to have a whole person.

"Jim, even if I never see you again, please try and forgive Ria. And please try and forgive Edith. They both love you so much. They both want so much for you to be happy and at peace with yourself. Please try to understand that both of them are human, just like you are human. Just like we all are human. And we all make mistakes. And if, after making those mistakes, we try to make amends, we should be allowed to. You are not God, Jim. And neither are you a person without love and sensitivity and compassion. In fact, I have never known anyone more sensitive and more compassionate than you.

"That's why I love you. That's why I feel like I'm leaving half of myself behind when I walk out of this apartment. But I can't live with your hate, Jim. I can't live in fear. I love you so much. Loralee."

I read the letter over and over until my eyes blurred with tears. I felt hollowed out, weak and numb.

Deep inside I could hear the raging voice of a small, crying child . . . a voice that kept repeating, *She can't understand what they did to you. . . . Nobody can understand what they did to you.* . . . But from another part of my mind came a great silence. And I knew it was the sound of me without Loralee. And it grew louder and louder, until I could not hear the child anymore.

I spent that night more alone than I had ever believed I could be. The scent of her was still there, to remind me that she was gone. I drank coffee and paced as I thought and thought about what was happening. I ran through the entire experience with Ria, the good, the bad, the absurd. I read and reread Edith's letters. And then I read and reread Loralee's.

I never felt the urge to open a bottle and drown these things out. Instead I felt a compelling force well up inside me—a force that left me standing strong, with both feet firmly planted, ready to face what for two years I had been unwilling to face . . . until Loralee.

Now I knew I had been listening too much and too long to the hurt child. And now I had to be deaf to him. Before he buried me. Before he destroyed what I now knew was the most important thing. I only hoped I still had the strength to do it . . . to shut out forever his pitiful little soul that had screamed so loud, so long.

Daylight came slowly that Sunday. The fog was an enemy that did not want to retreat. I sat at my worktable, wondering how I should do what I had to do. I wanted to call Loralee and tell her it was all right. That it was over now. But I did not know where to call. And I knew that words alone were not going to suffice. She would need more than just words.

A faint knock sounded on my door. At first I thought I had imagined it. But then it sounded again. When I turned the door handle, Toby pushed his nose against the wood and bounded in. Loralee stood outside, the sea wind whipping her hair. Her eyes were red from crying. I opened the door all the way and looked at her. Her features were strained and drawn. She looked very frightened and very sad. "I didn't have any place to go," she said, still standing outside, her hands tucked inside her old navy pea coat. As she spoke, her eyes searched mine, as though her statement was really a question.

"You were right to leave," I said. "You were right to say what you said in your letter."

The wind whipped her hair around her face, covering her nose and mouth, then blew it back across her shoulder.

"What are we going to do, Jim?" she said, still not moving.

"We're going to stay together. Last night, I found out how to do that. I finally found out what I have to do."

"You did?"

"I did."

"Will you tell me, Jim? I need to have you tell me."

I looked at her and nodded and held out my hands. She slowly pulled her hands out of her pockets and placed them in mine. I pulled her to me and hugged her . . . held her. The emotion that was surging through me passed on into her. I told her of the raging little child and what I had to do to him.

She looked up at me, tears running down her cheeks. "I wish I could have known that child, Jim. I'm so sorry for him. I wish I could have held him and loved him and protected him."

"It would have made him very, very happy," I said, tears now in my own eyes. "He would have loved you so, so much."

In the next few days Loralee and I drew closer than ever. Now that we both understood the nature of my struggle, we were able to work at it together. Not that the voice of the child was silenced forever. But now, when he tried to scream out, both of us knew where the scream was coming from and that we could best control it by directly confronting it.

Not surprisingly, my relations with Ria got better and easier now. I still scoffed at her grandiose lifestyle, but now I could criticize without condemning. Still, I remained very wary of Ria. And she, to a degree, remained wary of me. We communicated mostly by telephone, a method which seemed to suit both of us. I no longer cared so deeply about having her tape-record "the story," and neither did I care much about being with her, particularly when Loralee would be there too. Sometimes I caught myself feeling jealous when the two of them were together—and sometimes I felt Ria being jealous of Loralee. Either way I was uncomfortable, and felt that was best dealt with by distance.

More and more Loralee and I were planning for our future. Whenever possible, she joined me on assignments that involved long trips by car, especially those that took us into northern California, whose clear streams and evergeen-covered mountains reminded us both of home. One such assignment took us into the High Sierras and then back across the state to the coast highway that led to Big Sur. We lingered in Big Sur two days, walking among the trees through which the sun's light filtered down in misty, golden streams. We sat mesmerized for hours by a waterfall, sad to think that soon we would have to return to the city.

We talked of North Carolina, and I told her again of the little farm where a creek of crystal water ran cold and sweet a stone's throw from the front porch of the old log cabin.

"Can we really go back and live there, Jim?" she asked. "Can we?"

And as I hugged her to me and murmured yes, I hoped I was not telling her a lie. Two considerations stood between us and the cabin. One was money. If we were to realize our dream of a family and a different kind of work, we had to carry a sizable nest egg back to North Carolina with us. And the nest egg was not sizable at this point.

But as important was the other consideration. Edith. If we moved back there, she would be part of our lives. She had her own cabin on that land, and she stayed in it every year from June until October.

And I was still not sure where my feeling lay with Edith. As with Ria, dealing with the screaming little boy had tempered much of my violent feelings toward Edith. And this had been helped along by more letters from her, and phone conversations with her, in which she talked more and more about hoping we could be close, that I was all she had in this world, and that my happiness meant so much to her. I wanted so much to believe her. But I doubted she could change so much in such a short time. I still could not completely transcend the feeling that she had robbed me of so much.

The summer of 1975 was upon us now, and the life that Loralee and I shared was smoothing out. We had begun putting money aside for our dream, but we were also enjoying the life we had to the fullest. Loralee and I traveled together, and she was with me when I played the role of a reporter in the film starring Arnold Schwarzenegger, *Pumping Iron;* I was interviewing him for a piece on the revival of body building in America. It was all fun, all the more so because we were in love.

Then the summer was violently interrupted. First, a routine Pap smear came back with a nonroutine reading. The gynecologist performed some further tests and the results were not good. Loralee had a cancerous condition of the uterus. There was a

210

chance the uterus could be saved, she was told, but surgery was required. The operation was performed, but another six weeks had to pass before the doctor could test to see if it had been a success. We waited. The test was made. The operation had not succeeded. Another operation was scheduled.

We clung to each other during this time, fearing the worst. Paranoia beset us. We wanted very much to have children, and that dream was hard to part with. But, although we tried not to think about it, our children's lives were not the only ones at stake. We talked around it at first and then faced it. We were both terrified. Because when you've never dealt with it before, cancer rhymes with death.

The second operation was performed as soon as possible, and then we waited again for the results. One morning I received a letter from *True* magazine—because of financial difficulties, they were dropping all contributing editors. That was $12,000 a year that we had planned on for our return to North Carolina.

The loss of the *True* income also forced us to move immediately from Malibu. Loralee's modeling career had bogged down, and there was only the *Times*'s salary keeping things afloat. Fortunately, we found a small house in Laguna Beach, only two blocks from the ocean, for half the Malibu rent.

By this time the tests on Loralee's second operation were made and the results came back. The news was good. The condition had not reappeared. We wept in relief, but we also knew that the shadow of the disease would mark us for the rest of our lives. There would always be a chance, however slim, of recurrence.

We received nothing but encouragement from Ria during this time. And from Edith, as well. Indeed, I had almost forgotten the hostilities that, only six months before, had nearly destroyed me. Because we lived seventy miles away from her now, we seldom saw Ria. And when we did, the time spent together was increasingly better. As for Edith, her letters were all positive, hopeful. She even made a gift that meant a great deal to me— twenty-two acres in the Blue Ridge Mountains.

After Loralee's recuperation, she tried to reenter modeling, but we were too far from Los Angeles, where all the action was.

We were still clinging to our dream, though, and to help in that direction, she took a job as a waitress at one of the better Laguna Beach restaurants. Every penny she made, she placed in a savings account.

As for me, my desire to live smog-free was taking its toll. I was commuting a hundred miles per day and by the time I reached home each evening, there was not enough of me left to wait up for Loralee's arrival from work. I was also still working on the movie treatment I had undertaken. Now more than ever I needed the extra money it might bring. The result of all this was that Loralee and I saw less and less of each other.

We saved every cent we could. And we began to plot and plan the quickest way to make a move. I worked feverishly on the movie treatment, spending all my days off on the project. It was the most immediate hope we had. The effort failed. In the eleventh hour of negotiations, the potential buyers, all of whom had been very optimistic, sent back the final word: no deal.

Loralee and I were both crushed. The cushion that we had counted on was not going to be there. And because of that, I was visited by another bout of insanity. Very soon I found myself in a strong disagreement with my editor at the *Times*. I could not afford to quit just then, but I sought and got a transfer to the Orange County edition of the paper. The Orange County office was convenient—only thirteen miles from our Laguna Beach home. In terms of serious journalism, however, the move was mad. When you wrote for the Orange County edition, your borders were Orange County. When you wrote for the downtown edition, your borders were the world. I was also out of place in the office. The young writers were waiting for "the big break," and the other ones considered themselves out to pasture. Since I was neither, I was in limbo. The "zone edition" mentality stripped me of my ambition, and I wondered what had happened to my desire to be the best.

I had known for a long time that I ought to leave journalism. At other papers I had grown bored quickly, but I'd thought that was because I wanted to work at a better paper. Now I had just walked away from a desk in the city room of the *Los Angeles*

Times. I was in the wrong game and I knew it. So why had I stuck with it so long—just to prove something to the nay-sayers who'd said I'd never succeed?

But if I was in limbo, Loralee was in hell. To her, waitressing was a nightmare of raving chefs, slave-driving owners, back-stabbing coworkers, and customers who undertipped and over-complained. She arrived home so tired and exhausted that it was at least an hour before she could relax enough even to smile.

By the spring of 1976 we were numb from it all. When June came, we decided to take a week's vacation to ease the pain. I wanted Loralee to actually see the place in North Carolina. I wanted her to know it was not just a dream—that it really did exist. As we made plans for this trip, for the first time in what seemed a very long time, we felt very, very good.

And Ria was part of that good feeling. I had told her we were taking the trip and she invited us to join her for a weekend before we left. Her new husband was in Europe for a month.

We reached her home on a Saturday morning. Loralee, her muscles and nerves tight from waitressing, excused herself short-ly after we arrived and went for a long swim in the pool. Ria and I sat at the kitchen table and talked.

"I can't get over how much that girl has changed you, Jim," she said.

I smiled and shrugged. "I know. You've said that before."

"No," she said, her face serious. "I really mean it, darling. She's . . . well, lately I have been having some rather strange and psychically powerful dreams about the two of you. I keep seeing this one moment where you and I are standing apart and glaring at each other. And from nowhere, she comes between us."

Ria's eyes closed and her head tilted back. Her body gave a great shiver. "And then," she said, "she reaches her hands out, taking my hand and yours in hers and pulling us to her."

Ria's voice was almost a whisper now. Another shiver. Her eyes opened and her head fell forward again. She rubbed her arms, smoothing away goosebumps. "Anyway," she smiled, her voice returning to its natural state, "she is the only person, apart from me, of course," she winked, "who understands you, who knows how to love you in the way that you need to be loved."

"Yeah," I said, stretching the word, "Loralee does do that."

"Does what?" came Loralee's voice. She had entered the house from the double doors that led out to the pool and, barefoot, had come upon us unnoticed.

"I was just agreeing with Ria," I said, pulling her towel-clad body to me, "that you're the best thing that's ever happened to me."

Loralee blushed.

"We mean that, dear," Ria said. "Now," she continued, becoming both businesslike and excited, "I want to take you two kids out tonight for an evening that you'll never forget. Loralee, I've had a special dress made for you, darling, and Veronica will be over in about an hour to fit it for you.

Loralee's eyes widened in surprise. "Ria, you didn't have to do that. . . . You shouldn't have!"

"Darling, I wanted to do it," Ria told her. "And you know, of course, whatever I want, I get."

"And then some," I said, rolling my eyes.

Ria laughed. "You should talk, Mr. Excessiveness."

"Like mother, like son," I said. "Like mother, like son."

Veronica came and went. I was not allowed to see Loralee's dress, so I took a book from the library and spent that time and most of the afternoon reading by the pool. Finally it was time to suit up for the evening. I came downstairs in my famous burgundy-and-black velvet tux with the frilly peach shirt and maroon, patent leather loafers. I went to the bar, made a drink, and was walking outside, enjoying the coolness of the early evening, when Ria's voice trumpeted, "Ta-daaaa!"

I turned and the two of them were standing, arm in arm, looking like two prom queens. Ria wore a shimmering, dark green gown cut low. Loralee was wearing a pink silk two-piece harem outfit. Smiling wickedly, she withdrew her arm from Ria's, and stepped toward me, swirling around ever so slowly. Because of a light behind her, I could see the outlines of her breasts and the shape of her body through the wispy material.

The evening that followed was elegant. I enjoyed every aspect of what I had before come to disdain—the fawning, the chitchat of table-visiting socialites . . . even, after several drinks, Ria's retelling of what now were very old stories, even to Loralee.

Loralee was radiant. When she left the table to go to the powder room, I saw that every male and female eye was on her as she moved . . . and she moved very well.

It was midnight before we finally reached Ria's home. I dropped the two of them at the front door and parked the Rolls out back in the garage. When I entered the house from the kitchen, I looked around and the two had disappeared. But soon they emerged, both wearing their nightgowns. "Get into a robe, kid," Ria said, "and join us in the library for a drink."

I went upstairs, changed, and came back down, stopping at the bar to pour some Kahlua. I found the two of them sitting on the floor in front of the fireplace, which already was aglow. "Sit down with us, Jim," Ria said, her blue eyes shimmering. "Here," she gestured, moving so that she was sitting close to Loralee.

I sat down beside her and Loralee and I turned so that we were facing each other with Ria in the middle. I sipped my drink, suddenly very aware of a vibration of togetherness that was coming from both of them.

"You know, Jim," Ria said, reaching her left hand to my head and stroking my hair, "this has been such a gorgeous, lovely evening for the three of us. It all goes along with a very strong, psychic feeling that I've been experiencing lately. I think you two will be very happy together," she said, her voice becoming low and melodic. "And because of your happiness together, I think I'll be happy with you, too."

She looked first at me, then at Loralee. She placed her arms around both of us and pulled us to her.

"Hold me," she said, in a little girl's voice. And we did.

The next week, after a farewell luncheon with Ria, we boarded a jet for the mountains of North Carolina. When we finally reached the cabin, after nearly an hour's drive east from the

Asheville-Hendersonville Airport, an almost surreal calm encompassed us. Neither of us spoke as we leaned against each other and absorbed the atmosphere. "My God," Loralee finally said, "I had forgotten there were so many shades of green."

For seven days we breathed pure air, drank chilled water from the spring, made love in the daylight on the bank of the creek, and slept close together, lulled by the coolness of the evening and the sound of the evening and the sound of water rolling over mossy rocks.

We took walks over the land, planning aloud some details of our dream. There, up from the cabin, would be our garden. And on the side of the mountain beyond it, we would keep bees, not just for honey but to pollinate the garden vegetables and the small orchard we envisioned. There, below the cabin, we would build my studio, where I would hang a sign that read "Writer in Residence."

During the evenings we talked about expanding the cabin—how great it would be to have a huge kitchen that opened out toward the garden and how the best place for the greenhouse, of course, would be the east side of the cabin, which got the most sun.

And then suddenly the seven days were up. We flew from Asheville to Atlanta, where we boarded the jet for L.A. In four hours we would be back in the world of reality again. As we sat in the terminal, we tried to be enthusiastic about the future. I was going to take another shot at the money in Hollywood, she was going to take some courses at Orange Coast Community College. But after we boarded the plane and were airborne, our talk petered out and finally we sat in silence.

When the big jet passed over Palm Springs and began its gradual descent toward Los Angeles International Airport, I leaned against Loralee and we both stared out her window at what we were heading back into. The sun had just settled into the Pacific and the afterlight illuminated the green-gray blanket of smog, causing both of us involuntarily to hold our breath. Then we were through the smog and saw, spread below us endlessly, eternally, millions of lights that, to us, illuminated nothing.

I settled back into my seat and, a moment later, she did the same. Then we both, in the same instant, turned to look at each other. The same thought was in both our minds. We had to get ourselves back home.

# Epilogue

January 1981, western North Carolina

We came here in October 1976, married for six months. The following July a son, James Strother, was born to us. Since the hour of his birth, I have understood love, and the ability to give and receive it, in a way that continues to amaze and delight me.

Because of my son I have learned, slowly, to look at my two mothers not as mothers, but as women, two human beings. Only since then have I been able to see them clearly. Only since then have I been able to accept them. Only since then have I been able to say honestly that neither of them meant me to have the childhood that has so plagued me.

That the birth of my son could bring this about is not a romantic oversimplification. I watched as he was delivered. Minutes later, he was placed in my arms. I looked at him and he looked at me. For one intense moment, we stared into each other's eyes. Then he smiled at me in a way I have never been smiled at before. Finally, I belonged.

Since that moment, I have been an observer of myself in change. I have felt the love of innocence, the love of belonging. And I have seen their power.

It is not a fragile thing, this love. For there have been some hard times since my son was born, times that made me so anxious and depressed that I withdrew from everyone. Everyone except him. Every time he has called, I have answered. Every time he has needed my attention, he has received it. There were times when I felt I had nothing to give to anyone, even him. Yet he showed me that I did. He still shows me that I can.

It is because of him that I have come closer and closer to being the whole man that I have needed so desperately to become. It is because of him that I have been able to soothe the raging child who, I regret, will always be a part of me.

I will always wonder what the real story of my birth was. There will never be an answer, and now it no longer matters.